SCHOLASTIC

GET READY FOR READING

DEVELOPING PHONOLOGICAL AWARENESS

- SONGS, RHYMES AND LISTENING GAMES ON 2 AUDIO CDS
- ACTIVITIES FOR EVERY LETTER SOUND
- PREPARE THE EARS, EYES AND BRAIN FOR READING

SHONA CARMICHAEL

Author
Shona Carmichael

Editors
Rachel Mackinnon, Simret Brar, Louise Titley

Assistant Editor
Margaret Eaton

Illustrations
Gaynor Berry

Series Designer
Anna Oliwa

Audio CDs
Sally Scott and Simon Anderson

Designed using Adobe InDesign

Published by Scholastic Ltd
Villiers House
Clarendon Avenue
Leamington Spa
Warwickshire CV32 5PR

www.scholastic.co.uk

Printed by Bell & Bain Ltd

1 2 3 4 5 6 7 8 9   8 9 0 1 2 3 4 5 6 7

Acknowledgements
The publishers gratefully acknowledge permission to reproduce the following copyright material:
British Council for the use of 'We're going to the zoo to see a kangaroo' © Cambridge English On-line (British Council LearnEnglish Kids www.britishcouncil.org/learnenglish/kids).
David Holmes for the use of the lyrics 'I'm a scary skeleton' by David Holmes © 2007, David Holmes.
Beverly McLoughland for the use of 'Annie, Annie' by Beverly McLoughland © 1993, Scholastic Collections.

British Library Cataloguing-in-Publication Data
A catalogue record for this book is available from the British Library.

ISBN 978-0749-85917-6

GET READY FOR READING: CONTENTS

GET READY FOR READING: CD TRACK LISTS

CD ONE: SONGS AND RHYMES

1. The Big Ship Sails
2. Bobby Shaftoe
3. Here's a Ball for Baby
4. Ride a Cock-Horse
5. There Was a Crooked Man
6. Diddle, Diddle Dumpling
7. Dance to Your Daddy
8. One Elephant Went Out to Play
9. Old Macdonald
10. The Farmer's in his Den
11. These are Grandma's Spectacles
12. Go to Bed, Tom
13. Goosey, Goosey Gander
14. A Hunting We Will Go
15. Hot Cross Buns!
16. Humpty Dumpty
17. If You're Happy and You Know It
18. In and Out the Dusty Bluebells
19. Jack Be Nimble
20. Jack and Jill
21. Lavender's Blue
22. Here We Go Looby Loo
23. Have You Seen the Muffin Man?
24. Here We Go Round the Mulberry Bush
25. This Old Man, He Played One
26. Oranges and Lemons
27. Polly Put the Kettle On
28. Half a Pound of Tuppeny Rice
29. Five Little Ducks
30. Round and Round the Garden
31. Row, Row, Row Your Boat
32. Simple Simon
33. Six Salty Sausages
34. Teddy Bear, Teddy Bear
35. Ten Little Men
36. Uncle Moon
37. Roses are Red
38. Incy Wincy Spider
39. Foxy's Hole
40. Yankee Doodle Dandy
41. Fuzzy Wuzzy Was a Bear

CD TWO: LISTENING GAMES

1. The a sound
2. The b sound
3. The c/k sound
4. The d sound
5. The e sound
6. The f sound
7. The g sound
8. The h sound
9. The i sound
10. The j sound
11. The l sound
12. The m sound
13. The n sound
14. The o sound
15. The p sound
16. The qu sound
17. The r sound
18. The s sound
19. The t sound
20. The u sound
21. The v sound
22. The w sound
23. The x sound
24. The y sound
25. The z sound

GET READY FOR READING
INTRODUCTION

WHY USE THIS BOOK?

This book is all about giving pre-school children a thorough preparation in phonics before they begin learning to read at school. The book aims to:

- teach phonological awareness (recognition of the sounds in words)
- cover the 25 basic sounds of the alphabet: a, b, c/k, d, e, f, g, h, i, j, l, m, n, o, p, qu, r, s, t, u, v, w, x, y and z.
- prepare the ears, eyes and brain for reading at primary school
- develop listening and speaking skills
- offer a wide variety of activities.

Research suggests that the peak period for language development in children is between birth and six years of age. With this knowledge, it seems sensible to assist in the development of language skills before children begin primary school.

Being able to listen to and identify alphabetical sounds is a vital pre-reading skill. For example, when a child hears and recognises the 'a' sound in a word such as apple, he or she is using phonological awareness. Phonological awareness is all about hearing, and is the stage before the seeing, reading and writing of letter shapes. The ability to distinguish between distinct sounds is vital; for example, a child should be able to hear and recognise the 'b' sound in bat, ball, rabbit and crab; and hear the difference between, for example, meat or neat, three or free, bill or pill.

After developing phonological awareness, children learn to associate the sound of a letter with the letter shape. This is called phonics (when a child looks at the shape of the letter a, and says the 'a' sound).

HOW TO USE THE BOOK

This book is structured as a 'dip in' resource. There is no rigid programme or order to follow, nor is there a correct time to begin teaching the material in this book, as this will depend on each child's/group's ability. However, it might be useful to bear in mind the following points:

- The simplest sounds for a child to make are a, b, c/k, d, e, i, m, n, o, p, t, u, w. These may be the best starting point.
- Then comes f, g, h, j, l, qu, r, s, v, y, x and z.
- The sounds x and z should be left until the other sounds have been completed. This is because many words for x and z do not all have the initial sound at the beginning, but the sound comes after the beginning of the word, as in mix and buzz.

The difficulty level of the activities remains the same for all the sounds in the book.

HOW THE BOOK IS ORGANISED

The book is divided into 25 sections (one section for each of the letter sounds of the alphabet). Each section is then divided into three areas or topics: Listening, Seeing and Thinking. At the end of each section there are four photocopiable sheets to use with the children.

1 LISTENING

Each listening section consists of the following:

- a pronounciation guide
- a selection of songs and rhymes (a CD icon indicates which ones are also on the audio CD – see page 6 for more information about the CD)
- a variety of activities
- an evaluation exercise
- an extension activity.

PRONOUCIATION GUIDE

For every sound there is a written description of how to make that sound.

NURSERY RHYMES AND SONGS

The selection of nursery rhymes and songs has been included because these encourage children to recognise rhyming sounds and similar sounding patterns in words. This is an important skill in learning to read.

Because young children learn partly through movement and touch (kinaesthetic learning style), it is important to try to include actions with the rhymes, whenever possible.

Adults can also help to emphasise rhyming – for example, by missing out the rhyming word in a familiar nursery rhyme for the child to complete, such as Jack and ___ went up the ___ .

THE AUDIO CDS

There are two audio CDs accompanying this book. The first CD consists of a total of 41 songs and rhymes, selected from the book. The songs and rhymes are shown by the CD icon. The second CD consists of 25 tracks. These are listening games for each letter sound of the alphabet. Each track consists of a set of questions and instructions for the children, which prompt them to identify certain objects, sounds or actions that relate to the particular letter sound in question.

The listening section in each chapter of the book also directs you to the listening games on the second audio CD. This section also provides you with the answers to some of the questions and instructions on the CD.

ACTIVITIES

There are a number of fun activities for every sound. These take the form of action games, listening games, guessing games and so on. All of these aim to encourage the children to listen to and identify the letter sound.

EVALUATION

At the beginning of the evaluation exercise, the children are asked to rub the outside parts of their ears. This is to stimulate the sensory parts of the ears, and to focus the children's minds to listening carefully. The evaluation consists of three hearing tasks that will enable adults to decide if the children can hear the sound. The same level of difficulty is maintained for all of the letter sounds.

EXTENSION ACTIVITY

The extension activity is for children who have successfully learned to recognise the letter sounds. It is quite a challenginng exercise involving 'robot talk' – the process of breaking words down into their individual sounds, with adult support.

2 SEEING

For each letter sound there are three photocopiable sheets that make up the topic of 'Seeing'. The first activity in this section asks the children to identify objects beginning with (or containing) the sound being studied. It helps the children to distinguish objects and hear the sound; this activity can be done alongside activities from the listening section. The other activities in this section include spot-the-difference and maze/map challenges.

Exercises such as these have been included because children benefit from activities that train the eyes to spot small differences in shapes and objects, thus helping them to differentiate between the letter shapes of the alphabet. The maze/map exercises encourage the development of coordinated eye movement from left to right for reading. This material provides excellent practice to train the eyes.

3 THINKING

The topic of 'Thinking' is divided into two parts. The first is a series of indoor and outdoor physical activities for the children to take part in. The second part is a list of questions relating to a photocopiable page with a particular scenario illustrated on it.

The physical activities are a mix of cross-lateral, balancing and coordination exercises. The activities also ask the children to use their imagination in conjunction with the physical exercises (for example, imagine you are a ball and bounce up and down). The physical activities are designed to stimulate both sides of the brain, with the ultimate aim of exercising the brain, thus preparing it for the challenges of learning pre-reading and reading skills.

In the second part of the thinking section, there is a list of questions that focus on an illustrated scenario (which is set out on a photocopiable page). The illustrations are designed to encourage children to think and to reason. The questions are open-ended. The activity always begins with easy literal questions, where the answer is in the picture. This gains the children's confidence. The level of questioning then moves on to encourage reasoning and thinking by asking about details that do not appear in the picture.

The questions given are a guide as to what may be asked, so you might need to change or adapt them according to the ability of each child/group with whom you are working. It might be useful to look at these 'thinking' photocopiables in groups, because when a group of young children discuss ideas together, a wider range of skills comes into play – skills such as:

- openness to new thinking and ideas
- respect for others, and for conflicting points of view
- skills in forming and communicating their own beliefs and view of the world
- the practice and building up of ideas
- thinking creatively and imaginatively.

EARLY YEARS GUIDELINES

Overall, this book has been developed to give the pre-school children in your setting the confidence to develop phonological awareness. It has been based on the Early Years Foundation Stage Guidelines (2006) which advises that early years educators should:

- provide time and opportunities for children to develop phonological awareness through small group and individual teaching;
- develop children's phonological awareness through games, music, songs and poetry;
- sing songs and play games that reinforce letter sounds;
- help children break down the sounds in words;
- help children build up the sounds in words.

THE a SOUND

(a as in apple)

PRONUNCIATION GUIDE

To make the sound **a**, open your mouth wide, and imagine a doctor is looking at your throat as you say aaaaaaaa.

LISTENING

WHAT'S ON THE CD

- The rhymes and games for the a sound include:
  - The Big Ship Sails
  - Listening game

RHYMES AND SONGS

- Share rhymes and songs containing the **a** sound.

A Hat for a Cat

Where are you going,
My little cat?

I am going to town,
To get me a hat.

What! A hat for a cat!
A cat get a hat!
Whoever saw a cat with a hat?

The Big Ship Sails

The big ship sails through the ally-ally-oh
The ally-ally-oh, the ally-ally-oh,
The big ship sails through the ally-ally-oh
On the last day of September.
Ally-ally-oh, ally-ally-oh,
The big ship sails away.
The big ship sails through the ally-ally-oh
On the last day of September.

Annie, Annie

Annie, Annie
Climbing trees,
Scrapes her elbows
Skins her knees,
Scuffs her shoes,
And snags her hair.
What's Annie doing
Way up there?

Annie, Annie
Says it's fun,
Climbing close
To the sun,
Far up where
It's grand to be,
As high as high
And swinging free.

An Apple a Day

An apple a day keeps the doctor away.
An apple in the morning – doctor's warning.
Roast apple at night – starves the doctor out right
Eat an apple going to bed – knock the doctor on the head.
Three each day, seven a week – ruddy apple, ruddy cheek.

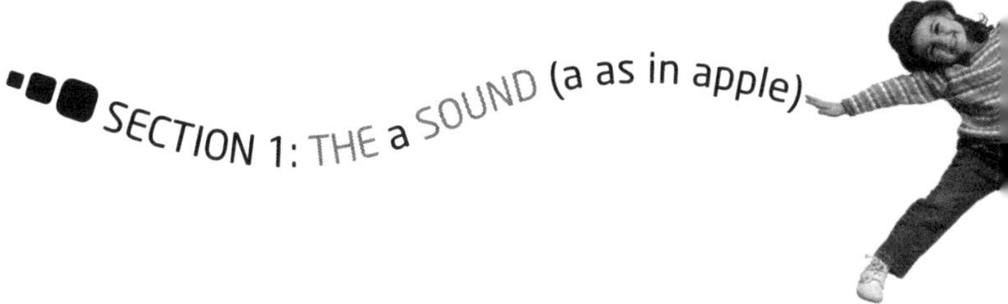

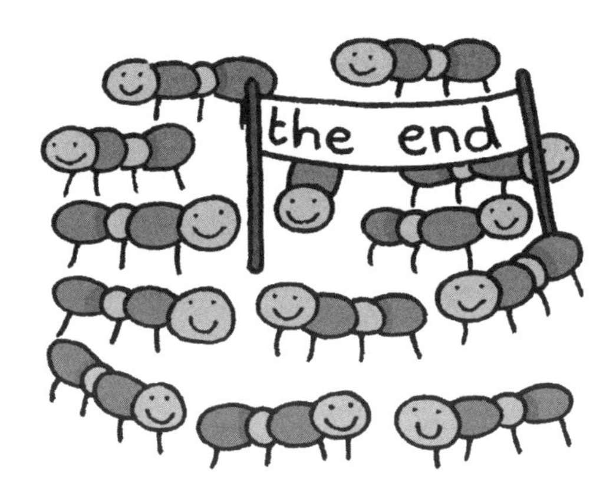

The Ants Go Marching

The ants go marching one by one, hurrah, hurrah
The ants go marching one by one, hurrah, hurrah
The ants go marching one by one,
The little one stops to suck his thumb
And they all go marching down to the ground
To get out of the rain, BOOM! BOOM! BOOM!

The ants go marching two by two, hurrah, hurrah
The ants go marching two by two, hurrah, hurrah
The ants go marching two by two,
The little one stops to tie his shoe
And they all go marching down to the ground
To get out of the rain, BOOM! BOOM! BOOM!

The ants go marching three by three...
The little one stops to climb a tree

The ants go marching four by four...
The little one stops to shut the door

The ants go marching five by five...
The little one stops to take a dive

The ants go marching six by six...
The little one stops to pick up sticks

The ants go marching seven by seven...
The little one stops to pray to heaven

The ants go marching eight by eight...
The little one stops to shut the gate

The ants go marching nine by nine...
The little one stops to check the time

The ants go marching ten by ten...
The little one stops to say 'THE END'

Old Noah

Old Noah once he built an ark,
And patched it up with hickory bark.

He anchored it to a great big rock,
And then he began to load his stock.

The animals went in one by one,
The elephant chewing a carroway bun.

The animals went in two by two,
The crocodile and the kangaroo.

The animals went in three by three,
The tall giraffe and the tiny flea.

The animals went in four by four,
The hippopotamus stuck in the door.

The animals went in five by five,
The bees mistook the bear for a hive.

The animals went in six by six,
The monkey was up to his usual tricks.

The animals went in seven by seven,
Said the ant to the elephant, 'Who're ye shov'n'?'

The animals went in eight by eight,
Some were early and some were late.

The animals went in nine by nine,
They all formed fours and marched in a line.

The animals went in ten by ten,
If you want any more you can read it again.

ACTIVITIES

Listen to the CD and ask the children if they can guess the missing words in the sentences. The sentences and answers are below.
- When I go to the zoo, I see all sorts of... (**animals**)
- When I go to the... I see lots of fish and different types of sea-life. (**aquarium**)

- Ask the children what other animal noises they can make. Play a sound game and ask the children to make the sound of an animal. See if an adult can guess what it is.
- Play an action game: an adult whispers an action to a child, remembering to emphasise the **a** sound. The child then has to act it out. Other children then try to guess the action. This is difficult, so give help and clues, so that the child is successful. Here are some examples of actions:
  - You are **asleep**.
  - You are **awake**.
  - Point to your **ankle**.
  - Pull up the **anchor** on a boat.
  - Shoot a bow and **arrow**.
  - Fall down. You have had an **accident**.
  - You are a policeman. Can you **arrest** a robber?
- Look for story books which begin with the **a** sound and read them aloud to your class. For example:

Aldo by John Burningham (Red Fox)
Alfie books by Shirley Hughes (Red Fox)
You're All Animals by Nicholas Allan (Red Fox)
Avocado Baby by John Burningham (Jonathan Cape Picture Books)
Amazing Grace by Mary Hoffman (Frances Lincoln Children's Books)

- Look for non-fiction books in the library. You could find books about animals, alligators and ambulances.
- Find children's names beginning with the **a** sound, such as Alan, Andrew, Adam, Abdul, Ann, Amelia, Amber, Abbie, Abeer.
- Use pictures from magazines and catalogues of things beginning with the **a** sound.
- Ask the children to look for **a** objects in their immediate environment. They could also do this when out and about (for example, at the supermarket). Play 'I Spy' with **a** words.

- Explain to the children that where they live is called their **address**. Ask them to find out their addresses.
- Buy a packet of **alfalfa** seeds. Ask the children to sprinkle some warm water on a piece of paper towel, and keep it damp. Then sprinkle some seeds on the paper. Encourage the children to find a warm place to put the seeds. The seeds should sprout very quickly.

EVALUATION

- These questions are intended to assess the children's ability to hear the **a** sound. Ask them to rub the outside part of their ears before they start to listen.
- Read the following questions to the children:

1. What sound is at the beginning of these words?
   ant, ankle, ambulance, apple, axe, arrow, anchor, alligator, anorak
2. In these groups of three words, which word begins with the **a** sound?
   a) ant, doll, lion
   b) nursery, animal, game
   c) book, alligator, pencil
   d) ambulance, friend, rattle
   e) dog, rocket, apple
   f) house, goat, arrow
3. Clap when you hear a word with the **a** sound at the beginning:
   apple, book, arrow, pen, dog, ant, alligator, cow, animal

EXTENSION ACTIVITY

- As a further challenge for children you can try 'Robot talk'. A list of suggested words is given below.
  - The adult says the word such as 'ant' and then says it in 'Robot talk' /a/n/t/, sounding out the

individual sounds. Then repeat this.

■ The child then says the word, for example 'ant'. It may take a few tries to perfect the word.

■ The adult then says the sounds and claps each one, for example /a/n/t/. Then the child joins in.

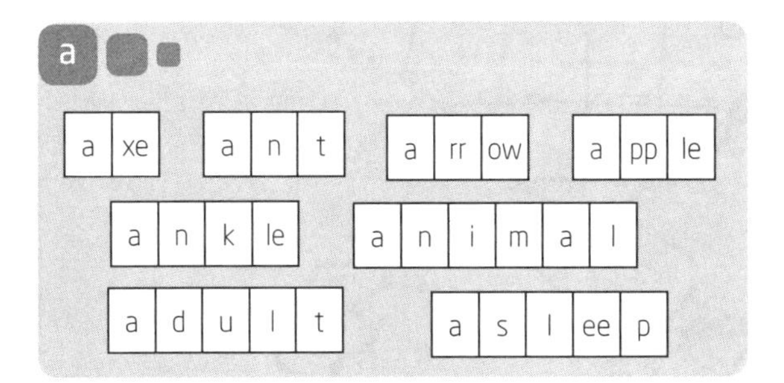

SEEING

■ Show the children photocopiable page 13 and ask them if they can identify the objects beginning with the **a** sound.

■ Make two copies of photocopiable page 13. Cut out the images and use them for games such as 'Snap' and 'Pairs'.

■ Show the children photocopiable page 14 and ask them to spot the differences between the two ambulances. Can they find all five things that are different in the second picture?

■ Display photocopiable page 15. Ask the children to help the ambulance reach the hospital, through the streets. They should trace the route with their finger, or use a pencil.. Encourage them to move their eyes from left to right as they complete the activity.

THINKING

■ Demonstrate lifting your right **ankle** and right hand. Then lift your left ankle and left hand. Encourage the children to join in. Once they have managed that, ask them to march around, lifting the opposite ankles and hands. This takes a lot of practice.

■ Ask the children to imagine they are carrying a giant **apple**. They should make a great big circle with one arm to carry the apple in, and then use the other arm. Next, ask them to try making big circles with both arms at the same time, following the circles with their eyes.

■ Invite the children to imagine they are **ambulance** drivers and they have to get a patient to the hospital as quickly as possible. What has happened to the patient? They should sound their siren to warn everyone that they are coming. Tell them to drive their ambulance carefully so that they do not have a crash and hurt anyone else.

■ Ask the children to imagine they are an **animal**. Ask: *What animal would you like to be? Can you move around like your animal? Can you make the sounds of your animal? What does your animal like to eat? Where does your animal like to sleep?*

THINKING AND REASONING SKILLS

■ Show the children the picture on photocopiable page 12 and ask them the following questions:

1. Who is in the picture?
2. What are they doing?
3. How does the anorak close?
4. Why do you think the boy is putting on an anorak?
5. Where do you think he is going?
6. What do you think the weather is like?
7. Why do you think that?
8. Is the boy happy or sad?
9. How do you know?
10. Where do you like to go?
11. What makes you feel happy?

Words beginning with *a*

Can you guess the word beginning with ***a***?

Answers: ant, ambulance, apple, axe, arrow, anchor

Spot the difference

Can you find five things that are different in the second picture?

Going to the hospital

Help the ambulance to reach the hospital, through the streets.
Follow the street with your finger or a pencil.

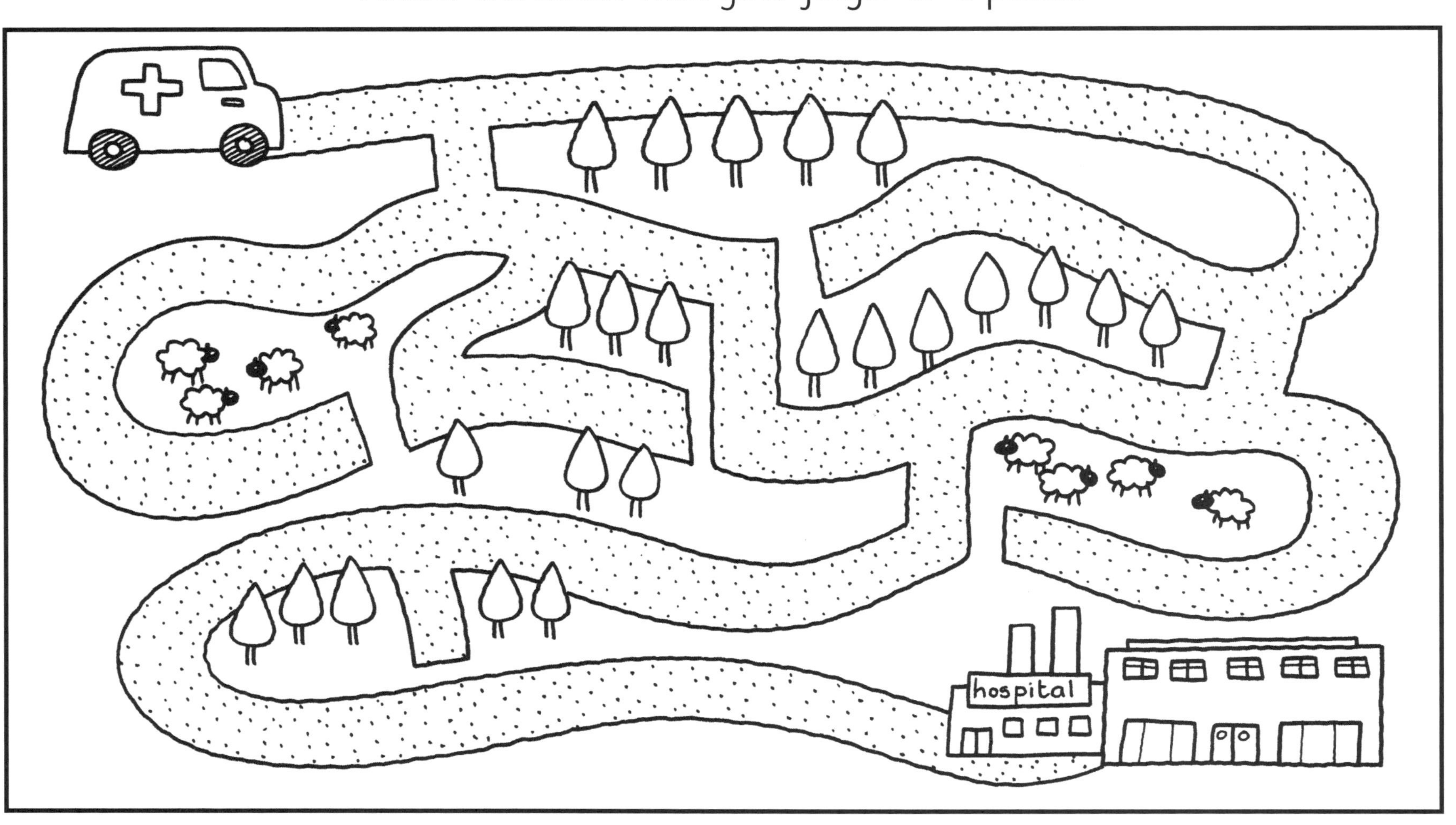

THE b SOUND

(b as in ball)

PRONUNCIATION GUIDE
To make the sound **b**, bring your lips together and then pop them open. Feel the air come out.

LISTENING

WHAT'S ON THE CD?

- The rhymes and games for the b sound include:
  - Bobby Shaftoe
  - Here's a Ball for Baby
  - Listening game

RHYMES AND SONGS

- Share rhymes and songs containing the **b** sound.

Bye, Baby Bunting

Bye, baby bunting
Daddy's gone a-hunting
To get a little rabbit skin
To wrap the baby bunting in.

Little Boy Blue

Little Boy Blue
Come blow your horn,
The sheep's in the meadow,
The cow's in the corn;
Where is the boy
Who looks after the sheep?
He's under a haycock
Fast asleep.
Will you wake him?
No, not I,
For if I do,
He's sure to cry.

Baa, Baa, Black Sheep

Baa, baa, black sheep,
Have you any wool?
Yes, sir, yes, sir,
Three bags full:
One for the master,
And one for the dame,
And one for the little boy
Who lives down the lane.

The Beehive

Here is the beehive, where are the bees?
(Put two hands together with fingers folded inwards.)
Hidden away where nobody sees.
Watch and you will see them come out of their hives,
One, two, three, four, five.
(Put fingers out one at a time when counting.)
Buzz, buzz, buzz.

Bobby Shaftoe

Bobby Shaftoe's gone to sea,
Silver buckles on his knee.
He'll come back and marry me,
Bonny Bobby Shaftoe!

Bobby Shaftoe's bright and fair,
Combing down his yellow hair;
He's my love for evermore,
Bonny Bobby Shaftoe.

Here's a Ball for Baby

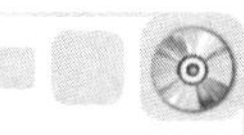

Here's a ball for baby, big and soft and round
(Make a round shape with your hands.)
Here is baby's hammer, see how he can pound.
(Lightly hammer using one hand.)
Here's the baby's music, clapping, clapping so
(Clap your hands.)
Here's the baby's soldiers, standing in a row.
(Hold up one hand, touching all the fingers.)
Here's the big umbrella to keep the baby dry
(Make an umbrella shape with both hands)
And here is baby's cradle, to rock the baby bye.
(Turn umbrella upside down to rock the baby in.)

Blow, Wind, Blow

Blow, wind, blow! And go, mill, go!
That the miller may grind his corn;
That the baker may take it,
And into bread make it,
And bring us a loaf in the morn.

ACTIVITIES

Listen to the CD. Ask the children if they can guess what the sound effects are.

- What is buzzing around the flowers? (**bee**)
- What is the person doing to the whistle? (**blowing**)
- Who is crying? (**baby**)

- Play an action game: an adult whispers an action to a child, remembering to emphasise the **b** sound. The child then has to act it out. Other children then try to guess the action. This is difficult, so give help and clues, so that the child is successful. Here are some examples of actions:
  - **Blow** up a **balloon**.
  - **Buzz** like a **bee**.
  - **Brush** the floor.
  - Give a dog a **bone**.
  - **Bounce** a **ball**.
  - Make a **bow**.
  - **Build** a tower of **bricks**.
  - Eat a **banana**.

- Feed a **baby** a **bottle**.
- **Bake** a cake.

■ Look for story books which begin with the **b** sound and read them aloud to your class. For example:

Brown Bear, Brown Bear, What Do You See? by Bill Martin, Eric Carle (Puffin Books)
Blue Rabbit and Friends; Blue Rabbit and the Runaway Bear by Christopher Wormell (Puffin Books)
We're Going on a Bear Hunt by Michael Rosen and Helen Oxenbury (Walker Books Ltd)
Bear Snores On by Karma Wilson and Jane Chapman (Simon & Schuster Children's Books)
Bad Habits! Or the Taming of Lucretzia Crum by Babette Cole (Hamish Hamilton Ltd)
Can't You Sleep, Little Bear? by Martin Waddell and Barbara Firth (Candlewick Press)
Bartholomew and the Bug by Neal Layton (Hodder Children's Books)
Be Gentle! (A Bartholomew Bear Book) by Virginia Miller (Walker Books Ltd)
Postman Bear by Julia Donaldson and Axel Scheffler (Macmillan Children's Books)
Snow Bears by Martin Waddell and Sarah Fox-Davies (Walker Books Ltd)

■ Look for non-fiction books in the library. You can find books about butterflies, boats, bears and babies.

■ Find children's names beginning with the **b** sound, such as Bobby, Brian, Barry, Billy, Basheer, Benjamin, Belinda, Brooke, Bridget, Brenda, Beth, Bathsheba.

■ Use pictures from magazines and catalogues of things beginning with the **b** sound. How many toys can the children think of that begin with **b**? (For example: ball, bricks, balloons.)

■ Ask the children to look for objects beginning with the **b** sound in their immediate environment. Visit a **bakery**, and look at the different **breads**. Try to taste as many breads as you can. (Check for food allergies before commencing this activity.)

■ Ask the children if they know the names of **baby** animals. For example: cow-calf, sheep-lamb, hen-chick, dog-puppy, cat-kitten, pig-piglet, horse-foal.

■ Invite the children to bring in some **baby** photographs of themselves. Display the pictures and ask the children whether or not they can guess who is who.

EVALUATION

■ These questions are intended to assess the children's ability to hear the **b** sound. Ask them to rub the outside part of their ears before they start to listen.

■ Read the following questions to the children:

1. What sound is at the beginning of these words?
   balloon, boat, bag, ball, bell, butterfly, banana, bee, bottle, baby
2. In these groups of three words, which word begins with the **b** sound?
   a) ball, game, pig
   b) make, boxes, pan
   c) fish, bag, sleep
   d) best, sing, get
   e) car, dish, bear
   f) mother, fun, boy
3. Clap when you hear a word with a **b** sound at the beginning:
   ball, kick, boat, coat, biscuit, butterfly, dog, banana

EXTENSION ACTIVITY

■ As a further challenge for children you can try 'Robot talk'. A list of suggested words is given below.

- The adult says the word such as 'bag' and then says it in 'Robot talk' /b/a/g/, sounding out the individual sounds. Then repeat this.
- The child then says the word, for example 'bag'. It may take a few tries to perfect the word.

■ The adult then says the sounds and claps each one, for example /b/a/g/. Then the child joins in.

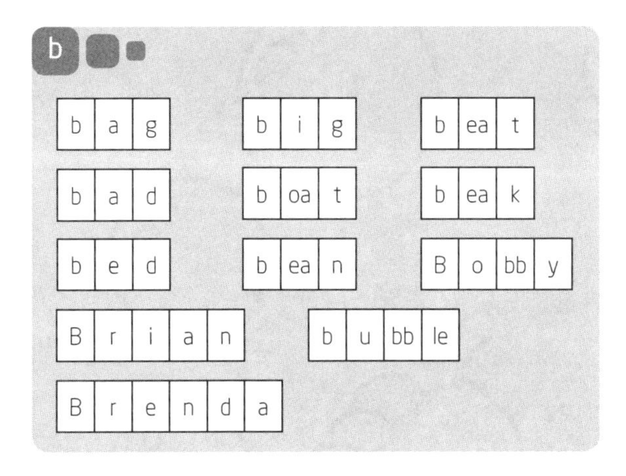

SEEING

■ Show the children photocopiable page 21 and ask them if they can identify the objects beginning with the **b** sound.
■ Make two copies of photocopiable page 21. Cut around the shapes and use them for games such as 'Snap' and 'Pairs'.
■ Show the children photocopiable page 22. Ask them to find the five differences in the second picture.
■ Display photocopiable page 23. Ask the children to join the matching pairs of objects, either by tracing a line with their finger, or using a pencil.

THINKING

■ Ask the children, in pairs, to throw a **ball** or a **beanbag** with little throws to each other. Invite them to try to catch it. Try throwing with one hand and then the other hand. Encourage them to follow the ball or beanbag with their eyes. They could then try kicking a ball, first with one foot, then with the other foot.
■ Draw a circle or use a hoop. Ask the children to throw a **ball** or a **beanbag** into the centre of the circle, using one hand, then the other hand. Remind them to keep their eyes on the ball.
■ Blow up **balloons** and challenge the children to not let them touch the ground. (Ensure that the children are supervised with balloons at all times.)
■ Use a **beanbag** to show the children how to pass it around your waist, using one hand to pass it to the other hand. Encourage them to try.
■ Ask the children to imagine they are a **ball**, and **bounce** around high and low; fast and slowly.
■ Encourage the children to imagine they are a **butterfly**, floating around gently, using their arms as wings.
■ Invite the children to pretend they are a **busy bumble bee**. Encourage them to fly around the flowers, collect the pollen and fly away again to the hive.
■ Pretend the class is having a **birthday** party. Ask the children: *Who will you invite? How many candles will you have on your cake? What favourite foods will you have? What games will you play? How will you feel when everyone sings? Do you like birthdays?*

THINKING AND REASONING SKILLS

■ Show the children the picture on photocopiable page 20 and ask them the following questions:

1. Who is in the picture?
2. What is she doing?
3. How many bubbles can you see?
4. Does she like blowing bubbles?
5. Why do you think that?
6. Have you ever blown bubbles in the air?
7. What are bubbles made of?
8. How do you blow to make bubbles?
9. How hard do you blow?
10. What shape are bubbles?
11. When is it hard to blow bubbles?
12. What colours are in bubbles?

Words beginning with *b*

Can you guess the word beginning with ***b***?

Answers: balloons, boat, bag, ball, bell, butterfly, banana, bee

Spot the difference

Can you find five things that are different in the second picture?

Match the objects

Can you match the drawings that are the same?
Use your finger or a pencil to draw a line between them.

THE c/k SOUND

(c as in **cat**, k as in **kite**)

PRONUNCIATION GUIDE

The sound **c/k** is made at the back of the mouth as air is forced over the back of the tongue. The tip of the tongue is at the back of the bottom teeth. Put your hand at your mouth to feel the air coming out.

LISTENING

WHAT'S ON THE CD

- The rhymes and games for the c/k sound include:
  - Ride a Cock-Horse
  - There Was a Crooked Man
  - Listening game

RHYMES AND SONGS

- Share rhymes and songs containing the **c/k** sound.

Cobbler, Cobbler

Cobbler, cobbler, mend my shoe.
Get it done by half-past two;
Stitch it up and stitch it down,
Then I'll give you half a crown.

Ride a Cock-Horse

Ride a cock-horse to Banbury Cross,
To see a fine lady upon a white horse;
Rings on her fingers and bells on her toes,
She shall have music wherever she goes.

Old King Cole

Old King Cole was a merry old soul,
And a merry old soul was he;
He called for his pipe,
And he called for his bowl,
And he called for his fiddlers three.

There Was a Crooked Man

There was a crooked man,
And he walked a crooked mile,
He found a crooked sixpence,
Against a crooked stile;
He bought a crooked cat,
Which caught a crooked mouse,
And they all lived together
In a little crooked house.

Cackle, Cackle, Mother Goose

Cackle, cackle, Mother Goose,
Have you any feathers loose?
Truly I have, pretty fellow,
Quite enough to fill a pillow.
Here are quills, take one or two,
And down to make a bed for you.

Hokey Cokey

You put your right arm in,
You put your right arm out
You put your right arm in,
And you shake it all about
You do the Hokey Cokey and you turn around
That's what it's all about.

Chorus:
Oh, Hokey, Cokey, Cokey! Oh, Hokey Cokey Cokey!
Oh, Hokey, Cokey, Cokey!
Knees bend, arms stretch.
Ra, ra, ra!

You put your left arm in...

You put your right leg in...

You put your left leg in...

You put your whole self in...

Clap, Clap Handies

Clap, clap handies
Daddy's coming home,
Pennies in his pocket
For his own wee boy/girl.

SECTION 3: THE c/k SOUND (c as in cat)

ACTIVITIES

Listen to the CD. Ask the children if they can guess what the sound effects are (the answers are given below).
- What is the person doing? (**coughing**)
- What are the people doing with their hands? (**clapping**)
- Which animal is making this sound? (**cat**)

■ Play an action game: an adult whispers an action to a child, remembering to emphasise the **c/k** sound. The child then has to act it out. Other children then try to guess the action. This is difficult, so give help and clues, so that the child is successful. For example, actions could include:
- **Catch** a ball.
- **Crawl**.
- **Clean** your teeth.
- **Climb** on a chair.
- **Call** out to a friend.
- **Cough**.
- **Creep** around.
- **Carry** a bag.
- Open the **curtains**.

■ Look for story books which begin with the **c/k** sound and read them aloud to your class. For example:

The Very Hungry Caterpillar by Eric Carle (Puffin Books)
Corduroy by Don Freeman (Puffin Books)
Cabbages and Kings by Elizabeth Seabrook and Jamie Wyeth (Viking Children's Books)
Creepy Castle by John Goodall (Ragged Bears)
Tom's Cat by Charlotte Voake (Walker Books Ltd)
Clown by Quentin Blake (Red Fox)
Katie Morag stories by Mairi Hedderwick (Red Fox)
Cats Sleep Anywhere by Eleanor Farjeon and Anne Mortimer (Frances Lincoln Publishers)
The Cat in the Hat by Dr Seuss (Collins)
A Cuddle for Claude by David Wojtowycz (Gullane Children's Books)

■ Look for non-fiction books in the library. You can find books about cars, cats and cookery.

■ Find children's names beginning with the **c/k** sound, such as Cameron, Connor, Karl, Kaleem, Kai, Caleb, Caroline, Katie, Caitlin, Kameela.

■ Make scrap books using pictures from magazines and catalogues of things beginning with the **c/k** sound.

■ Ask the children if they can **count** the numbers up to five. Can they count the numbers up to ten?

■ Ask the children to think of any vegetables beginning with the **c/k** sound (for example, **carrots**, **cauliflower**, **courgettes**). **Cut** fruit and vegetables into different shapes, such as melon into slices and balls, apple into slices or rings, courgette into slices or rings, celery into sticks, carrot into sticks or rings, cucumber into sticks or rings.

■ Use a **construction** set to make **cars** and a **castle**. Toy libraries often have construction sets.

EVALUATION

■ These questions are intended to assess the children's ability to hear the **c/k** sound. Ask them to rub the outside part of their ears before they start to listen.

■ Read the following questions to the children:

1. What sound is at the beginning of these words?
   cat, caterpillar, cake, candle, car, clown, camel, cow, carrot, camera
2. In these groups of three words, which word begins with the **c/k** sound?
   a) cow, bear, honey
   b) deer, rub, cap
   c) arm, candle, dog
   d) coat, farm, goat
   e) rabbit, hat, cat
   f) cup, get, game
3. Clap when you hear a word with a **c/k** sound at the beginning:
   candle, door, cup, cat, bag, caterpillar, house

EXTENSION ACTIVITY

■ As a further challenge for children you can try 'Robot talk'. A list of suggested words is given below.

- The adult says the word such as 'cat' and then says it in 'Robot talk' /c/a/t/, sounding out the individual sounds. Then repeat this.
- The child then says the word, for example 'cat'. It may take a few tries to perfect the word.
- The adult then says the sounds and claps each one, for example /c/a/t/. Then the child joins in.

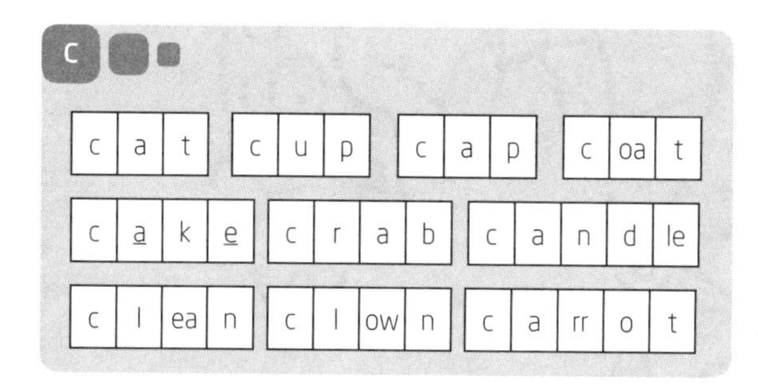

SEEING

■ Show the children a copy of photocopiable page 29 and ask them if they can identify the objects beginning with the **c/k** sound.

■ Make two copies of photocopiable page 29. Cut around the shapes and use them for games such as 'Snap' and 'Pairs'.

■ Ask the children to point to the clowns on photocopiable page 30.

■ Show the children photocopiable page 31. Invite them to help park the car using their finger or a pencil. Encourage them to move their eyes from left to right as they complete the activity.

THINKING

■ Ask the children to change hands while **cleaning** their teeth, using first one hand and then the other. Ask them to try to clean their teeth with their right hand, while bending their left leg at the knee. Then swap and brush teeth with the left hand, and bend the right leg at the knee.

■ Get the children to climb in and out of large **cardboard** boxes. Make the cardboard boxes into tunnels, and crawl through them.

■ Make a large cardboard box into a **castle**. Paint it on the outside and paint in windows and a door.

■ Encourage the children to try **catching** a ball or a beanbag. Tell them to make small upward throws at first to make this easier.

■ Ask the children to imagine they have a magic flying **carpet** and can fly around the room – waving to their friends below as they do this. Ask: *Where else would you like to fly to on the magic carpet? What would you do when you get there?*

■ Invite the children to imagine they have a very old **car**. Ask them to drive it around slowly, without bumping into anything – weaving in and out slowly, tooting the horn when they pass anyone. Then imagine they have a fast racing car. Can they make the engine noise? Tell them to race around in their fast car, without bumping into anything.

THINKING AND REASONING SKILLS

■ Show the children the picture on photocopiable page 28 and ask them the following questions:

1. Who is in the picture?
2. What do they have in their hands?
3. What are they wearing?
4. What do you think the clowns will do with the buckets of water?
5. Where do you think this is happening?
6. Why do clowns wear those outfits?
7. Who might be watching this?
8. Where might it be happening?
9. Will you laugh?
10. What would happen if you did this to an adult?
11. What would happen if you did this to a friend?
12. Would they be happy?
13. Would you like someone to do this to you?
14. How would you feel?
15. What would you do?

Words beginning with *c*

Can you guess the word beginning with **c**?

Answers: cat, caterpillar, cake, car, clown, camel, cow, carrot

Find the clown

Point to the pictures of the clowns.

Park the car

Help the driver to drive through the maze and park the car in the garage.
Use your finger or a pencil to drive the car through the streets.

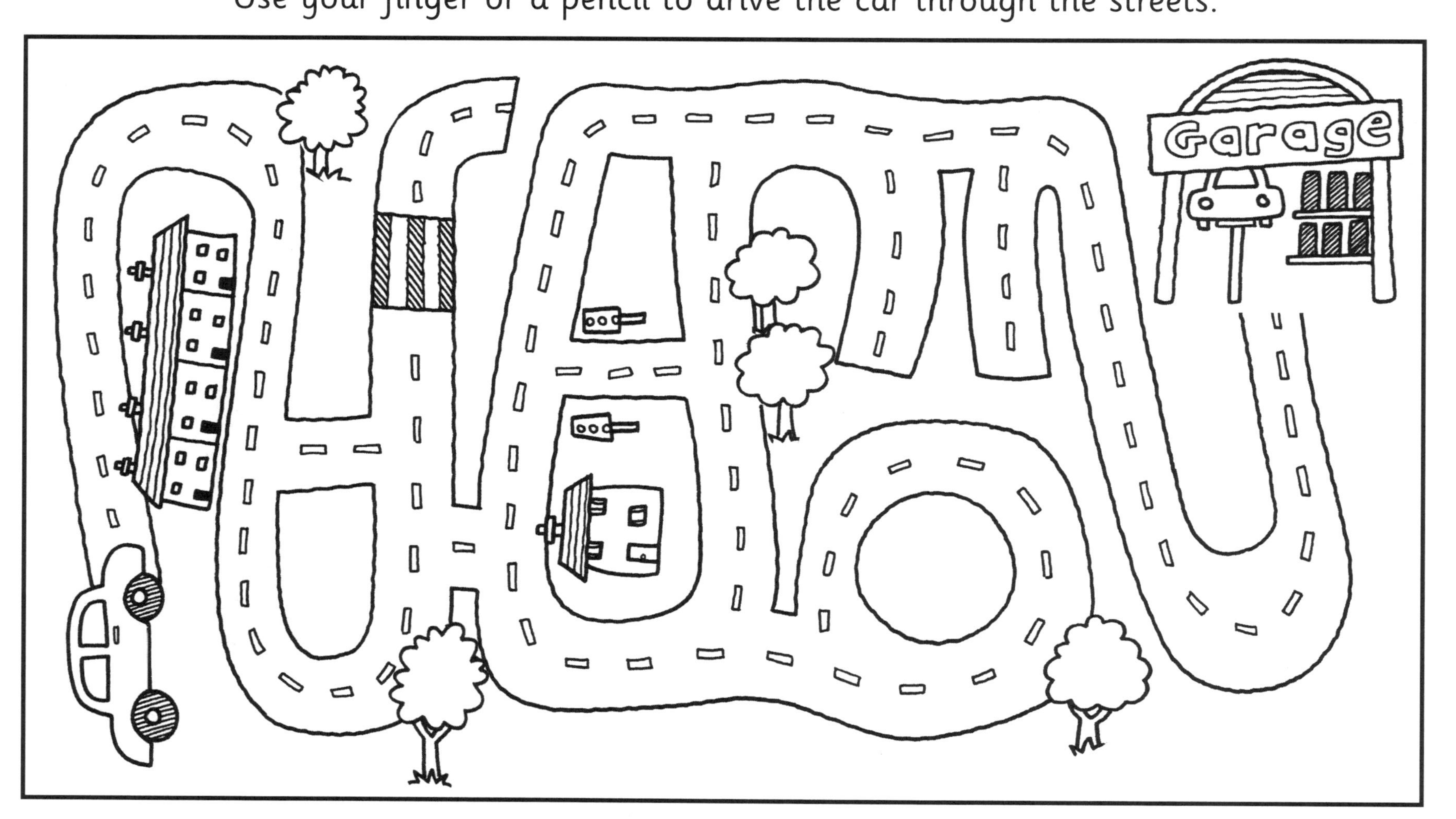

THE d SOUND
(d as in dog)

PRONUNCIATION GUIDE
To make the **d** sound, put the tip of your tongue behind your top teeth, and your tongue moves down while making the sound at the back of your mouth. You can feel the movement in the throat.

LISTENING

WHAT'S ON THE CD
- The rhymes and games for the d sound include:
  - Diddle Diddle Dumpling
  - Dance to your Daddy
  - Listening game

RHYMES AND SONGS
- Share rhymes and songs containing the **d** sound.

Ding, Dong, Bell

Ding, dong, bell
Pussy's in the well
Who put her in?
Little Johnny Flynn
Who pulled her out?
Little Tommy Stout
What a naughty boy was that
To try to drown poor Pussycat,
Who ne'er did any harm
But killed all the mice
In the farmer's barn!

Diddle, Diddle, Dumpling

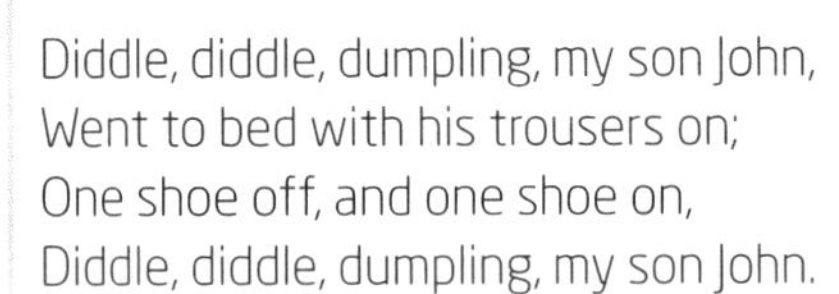

Diddle, diddle, dumpling, my son John,
Went to bed with his trousers on;
One shoe off, and one shoe on,
Diddle, diddle, dumpling, my son John.

Hey Diddle Diddle

Hey diddle diddle,
The cat and the fiddle,
The cow jumped over the moon;
The little dog laughed
To see such sport,
And the dish ran away with the spoon.

Do Your Ears Hang Low?

Do your ears hang low?
Do they wobble to and fro?
Can you tie them in a knot?
Can you tie them in a bow?
Can you throw them over your shoulder
Like a regimental soldier?
Do your ears hang low?

Dance to Your Daddy

Dance to your daddy,
My little babby,
Dance to your daddy, my little lamb;
You shall have a fishy,
In a little dishy,
You shall have a fishy,
When the boat comes in.

Dance to your daddy,
My little babby,
Dance to your daddy, my little lamb;
You shall have a fishy,
In a little dishy,
You shall have a fishy,
When the boat comes in.

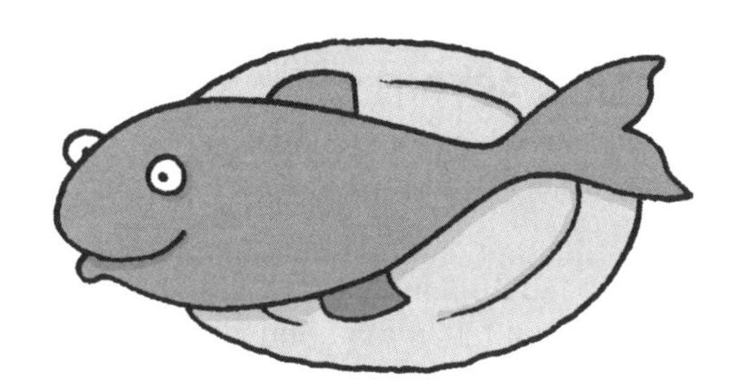

Miss Polly Had a Dolly

Miss Polly had a dolly,
Who was sick, sick, sick.
So she phoned for the doctor
To be quick, quick, quick.

The doctor came
With his bag and his hat,
And he rapped the door
With a rat-a-tat tat.

He looked at the dolly
And he shook his head.
Then he said 'Miss Polly,
Put her straight to bed.'

He wrote on a paper
For a pill, pill, pill.
'I'll be back in the morning
With my bill, bill, bill.'

Miss Polly actions

Verse 1: Children rock the dolly in their arms.
Verse 2: Children knock on an imaginary door.
Verse 3: Children shake their heads and wag their fingers.
Verse 4: Children pretend to write on a piece of paper.

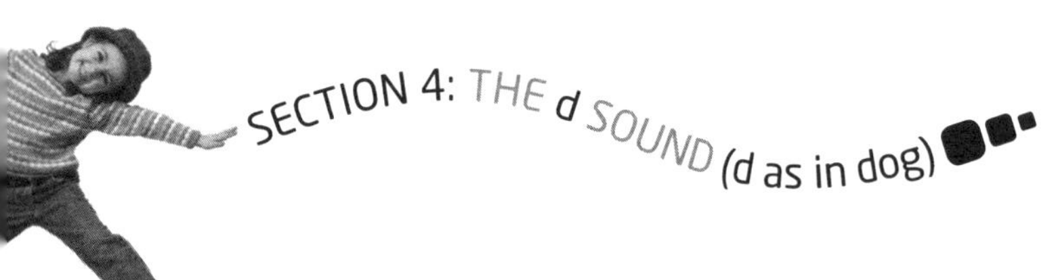

ACTIVITIES

Listen to the CD and ask the children if they can guess the following sounds:
- A **duck**
- A **dog**
- A **drum**

- Play an action game: an adult whispers an action to the child, remembering to emphasise the **d** sound. The child then has to act it out. Other children then try to guess the action. This is difficult, so give help and clues, so that the child is successful. For example, actions could include:
  - **Dig** a hole.
  - **Draw** a picture
  - **Drive** a car.
  - **Dance** around the room.
  - **Drop** a pencil.
  - Have a **drink**.
  - **Dive** into a pool.
  - Play a **drum**.
- Look for story books which begin with the **d** sound and read them aloud to your class. For example:

Doctor Dog by John Talbot (Hodder Wayland)
Dogger by Shirley Hughes (Red Fox)
Dad, I Can't Sleep by Michael Foreman (Andersen Press Ltd)
Dick Whittington (Ladybird Books)
Harry, the Dirty Dog by Gene Zion (Red Fox)
A Dark, Dark Tale by Ruth Brown (Red Fox)

- Look for non-fiction books in the library. You can find books about dogs, dinosaurs, dolls and Divali.
- Find children's names beginning with the **d** sound, such as David, Daniel, Darren, Duncan, Daleel, Doran, Dawn, Daisy, Dora, Donna, Diana, Deirdre, Dana, Daniella.
- Use pictures from magazines and catalogues of things beginning with the **d** sound.
- Ask the children to look for **d** objects in their immediate environment. They could also do this when they are out and about (for example, at the supermarket). Play 'I Spy' for **d** words.
- Learn about the Hindu festival of **Divali** together.
- Have the children been to a **dentist**? Explain that dentists look after our teeth. Make sure that the children know how to brush their teeth properly.

EVALUATION

- These questions are intended to assess the children's ability to hear the **d** sound. Ask them to rub the outside part of their ears before they start to listen.
- Read the following questions to the children:
  1. What sound is at the beginning of these words?
     dog, duck, doll, daffodil, donkey, doctor, dish, dinosaur, dragon, dentist
  2. In these groups of three words, which word begins with the **d** sound?
     a) dog, light, fish
     b) top, drink, gun
     c) pan, donkey, table
     d) boat, pen, dragon
     e) toy, father, duck
     f) doll, men, jelly
  3. Clap when you hear a word with a **d** sound at the beginning:
     dish, dog, apple, doctor, boat, duck, dinosaur, daisy

EXTENSION ACTIVITY

- As a further challenge for children you can try 'Robot talk'. A list of suggested words is given below.
  - The adult says the word such as 'dog' and then says it in 'Robot talk' /d/o/g/, sounding out the individual sounds. Then repeat this.

■ The child then says the word, for example 'dog'. It may take a few tries to perfect the word.

■ The adult then says the sounds and claps each one, for example /d/o/g/. Then the child joins in.

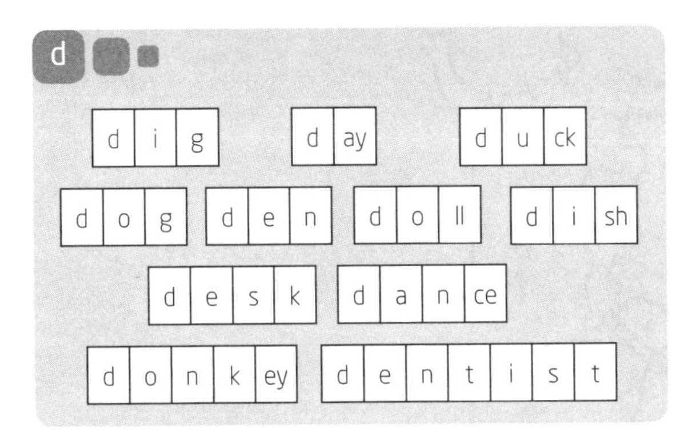

SEEING

■ Show the children photocopiable page 37 and ask them if they can identify the objects beginning with the **d** sound.

■ Make two copies of photocopiable page 37. Cut around the shapes and use them for games such as 'Snap' and 'Pairs'.

■ Can the children spot five differences in the second picture on photocopiable page 38?

■ Show the children photocopiable page 39. Can they put the three pictures in the right order? Can they tell a story with them?

THINKING

■ Show the children a **diamond** shape. Ask them to draw a big diamond in the air with one hand. Try this a few times. Then ask them if they can use their other hand to draw the diamond shape.

■ Say the nursery rhyme **Humpty Dumpty**. While you are saying it, **draw** a big wall in the air together. Use one hand, then the other, then with two hands clasped together.

■ Share the nursery rhyme **Ding, Dong, Bell**. While you are saying it, ask the children to draw a big Z shape in the air with one hand. Ask them to use the other hand, then both hands together.

■ Give the children chalk to **draw** large **diamond** shapes on the ground. Make a game, jumping in and out of the diamonds.

■ Find some cones, and get the children to practise **dribbling** a ball around them.

■ Together, look for **daisies** in the grass. Help the children to make daisy chains. (Check first that no children suffer from hayfever.)

■ Encourage the children to imagine they are a big, tall **daddy**. Walk around taking big steps, saying 'Hello' to their friends in a deep, daddy voice. Encourage them to draw a picture of a daddy.

■ Tell the children to pretend they are are a **doctor**. They have come to visit a **dolly**, who is sick. Ask: *What will you do? What will you say?*

■ Invite the children to imagine they are a **dinosaur**. Tell them to make big noises to scare everyone away and chase their friends, but do not touch them or hurt them – be kind and gentle, with a big voice.

THINKING AND REASONING SKILLS

■ Show the children the picture on photocopiable page 36 and ask them the following questions:

1. Who is in the picture?
2. What are they doing?
3. Where is this happening?
4. What is on the donkey's back?
5. What would you want to do if you were there?
6. How would you feel if you got a ride on the donkey?
7. How would you feel if you did not get a ride on the donkey?
8. What would you say and do?
9. Have you had a donkey ride?
10. How did it feel?
11. Were you frightened?

Words beginning with *d*

Can you guess the word beginning with ***d***?

Answers: dog, duck, doll, daffodil, donkey, dish, dinosaur, dragon

Spot the difference

Can you find five things that are different in the second picture?

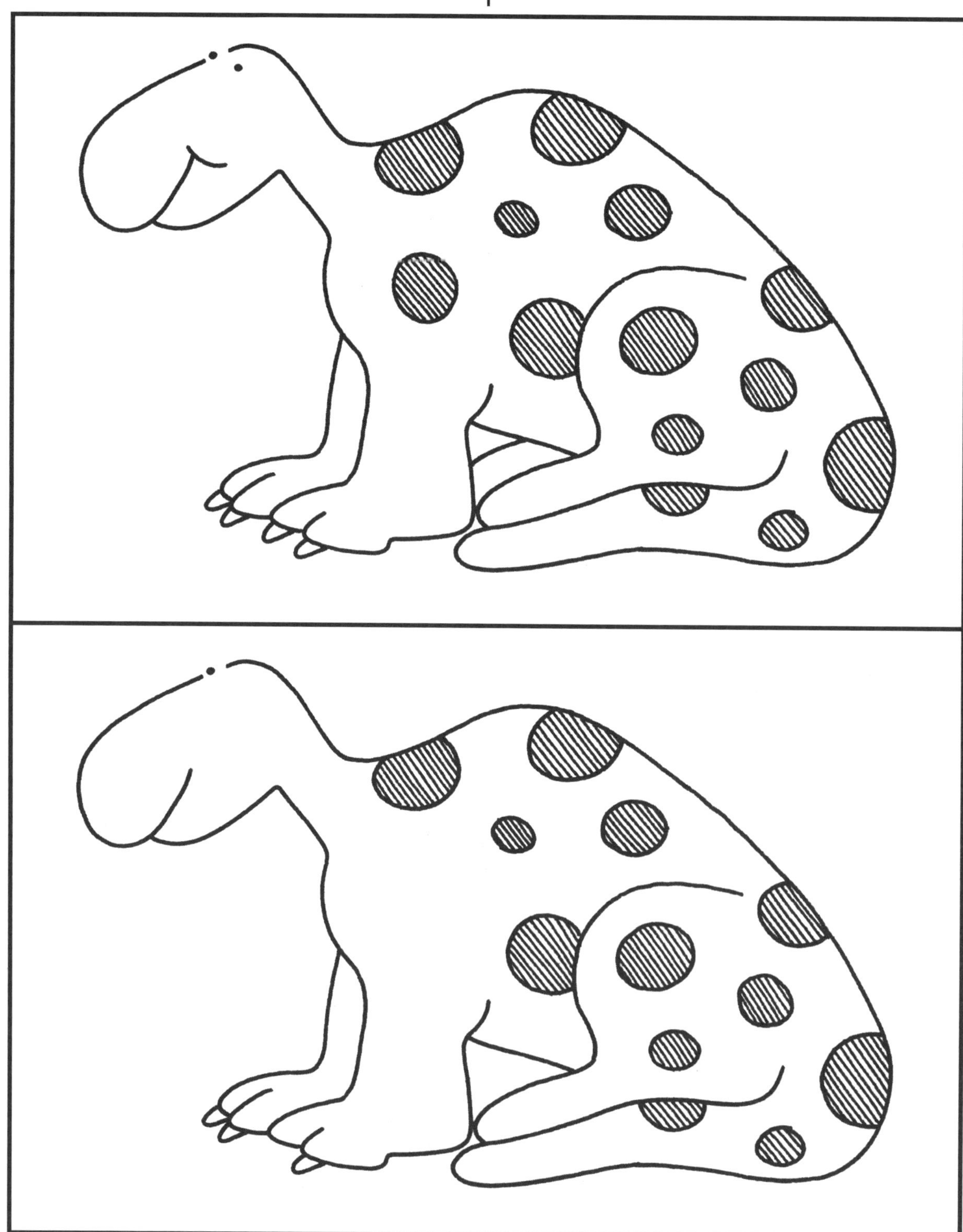

Picture sequence

Which picture comes first? Tell the story from the pictures.

THE e SOUND

(e as in egg)

PRONUNCIATION GUIDE

To make the **e** sound, the mouth is opened partially and air is passed over the tongue, making an *eh* sound.

LISTENING

WHAT'S ON THE CD

- The rhymes and games for the e sound include:
  - One Elephant Went out to Play
  - Listening game

RHYMES AND SONGS

- Share rhymes and songs containing the **e** sound.

Have You Ever in Your Long Legged Life

Have you ever, ever, ever, in your long legged life
Met a long legged sailor with a long legged wife?
No, I never, never, never, in my long legged life
Met a long legged sailor with a long legged wife.

Have you ever, ever, ever, in your short legged life
Met a short legged sailor with a short legged wife?
No, I never, never, never, in my short legged life
Met a short legged sailor with a short legged wife

then
...pigeon toed life...
...bow legged life...
...spoon headed life...

The Elephant

An elephant goes like this and that.
He's terrible big,
And he's terrible fat,
He has no fingers,
And he has no toes,
But goodness gracious, what a nose!

Elsie Marley

Elsie Marley is grown so fine,
She won't get up to feed the swine,
But lies in bed till eight or nine.
Lazy Elsie Marley.

One Elephant Went out to Play

One elephant went out to play,
On a spider's web one day,
He had such enormous fun
He asked another elephant to come.

Two elephants went out to play,
On a spider's web one day,
They had such enormous fun
They asked another elephant to come.

Three elephants went out to play,
On a spider's web one day,
They had such enormous fun
They asked another elephant to come.

Four elephants...

If You Ever

If you ever ever ever ever ever
If you ever ever ever meet a whale
You must never never never never never
You must never never never touch its tail;
For if you ever ever ever ever ever
If you ever ever ever touch its tail.
You will never never never never never
You will never never meet another whale.

Early to Bed

Early to bed,
Early to rise.
Makes little Jonny,
Wealthy and wise.

Early in the Morning

Early in the morning at about eight o'clock,
You can hear the postman's knock.
Up jumps Elly to open the door,
One letter, two letters, three letters,
Four.

ACTIVITIES

Listen to the CD and ask the children if they can guess the missing words in the sentences. The sentences and answers are below.
- For breakfast I like to eat scrambled... (**eggs**)
- All trains and cars have... (**engines**)
- An animal with a great big trunk instead of a nose is called an... (**elephant**)

■ Play an action game: an adult whispers an action to a child, remembering to emphasise the **e** sound. The child then has to act it out. Other children then try to guess the action. This is difficult, so give help and clues, so that the child is successful. For example, actions could be:
- **Enjoying** yourself.
- Being **excited** about a present.
- **Exploring** the jungle.
- **Escaping** from an **elephant**.
- **Exercising**.
- Eating an **egg**.

■ Look for story books which begin with the **e** sound and read them aloud to your class. For example:

The Elves and the Shoemaker (Ladybird Tales or Ready to Read)
Elmer stories by David McKee (Andersen Press)
The Enormous Turnip (Ladybird Tales and others)
The Emperor's New Clothes by Hans Christian Andersen (Ladybird Books)
The Elephant and the Bad Baby by Elfrida Vipont and Raymond Briggs (Puffin Books)
The Story of Babar, the Little Elephant by Jean de Brunhoff (Random House Children's Books)

■ Look for non-fiction books in the library. You can find books about birds and their eggs, elephants, and different kinds of engines

■ Find children's names beginning with the **e** sound, such as Eric, Edward, Elliot, Evan, Efraim, Ezra, Emily, Eleanor, Ella, Elspeth, Erin, Esther, Eriana.

■ Make scrap books using pictures from magazines and catalogues of things beginning with the **e** sound.

■ Collect **envelopes** from home for the recycling bin at the setting. Find different sizes and colours of envelopes, and paste them onto a big sheet of paper. Look at the writing on the envelope, and the stamps. Why do we use stamps?

■ At Easter, make Easter **eggs**. Boil the eggs until they are hard, and then paint the shells with bright colours. Some children roll their eggs down a hill on Easter morning. Tell the class that this symbolises, as Christians believe, rolling away the stone from Jesus' tomb on Easter morning.

■ The children can try beating **eggs** with a whisk to make them fluffy and add milk and butter to make scrambled eggs. (To be cooked by an adult.)

EVALUATION

■ These questions are intended to assess the children's ability to hear the **e** sound. Ask them to rub the outside part of their ears before they start to listen.

■ Read the following questions to the children:

1. What sound is at the beginning of these words?
   egg, elephant, elf, engine, elbow, envelope, escalator
2. In these groups of three words, which word begins with the **e** sound?
   a) egg, crisps, bank
   b) fire, neck, engine
   c) foot, elephant, game
   d) elf, mouse, fish
   e) nose, rose, end
   f) exercise, house, tree
3. Clap when you hear a word with the **e** sound at the beginning:
   elephant, egg, bowl, eggcup, mouse, elf, exercise, lion

EXTENSION ACTIVITY

■ As a further challenge for children you can try 'Robot talk'. A list of suggested words is given below.

- The adult says the word such as 'end' and then says it in 'Robot talk' /e/n/d/, sounding out the individual sounds. Then repeat this.
- The child then says the word, for example 'end'. It may take a few tried to perfect the word.
- The adult then says the sounds and claps each one, for example /e/n/d/. Then the child joins in.

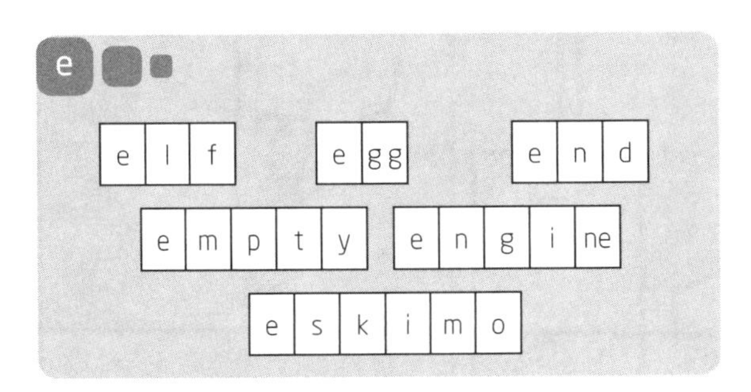

SEEING

■ Show the children photocopiable page 45 and ask them if they can identify the objects beginning with the **e** sound.

■ Make two copies of photocopiable page 45. Cut around the shapes and use them for games such as 'Snap' and 'Pairs'.

■ Hand out photocopiable page 46. Ask the children to circle or colour in the odd one out in each row.

■ Provide the children with photocopiable page 47. Ask them to join the dots to make the shape of an elephant.

THINKING

■ Ask the children to roll down a hill as though they are Easter **eggs** (ensure the area is safe before doing this). Tell them to roll slowly at first, and then roll as fast as they can.

■ Encourage the children to jump up and down, up and down, or run around until they are tired. Tell them this is called **exercise**, and that it is very good for you. What has happened to their breathing? Can they feel their hearts beating?

■ If you have a trampoline, encourage the children to **exercise** on it safely.

■ Make an **exercise** circuit with small fences (as at a horse show). You can use cardboard boxes for the jumps. Encourage the children to imagine they are a beautiful horse. Trot around, jumping over the fences, snorting with happiness.

■ Tell the children to imagine they are an **elephant** with an huge trunk. They should walk around with big, heavy steps, waving their trunk. Ask them to pretend they have a little baby elephant and gently touch it with their trunk.

■ Encourage the children to pretend to be a fire **engine**, racing (carefully) to the fire using their sirens, and then using a hose to put out (**extinguish**) the fire.

THINKING AND REASONING SKILLS

■ Show the children the picture on photocopiable page 44 and ask them the following questions:

1. What is happening in the picture?
2. Look at the egg timer. What does this tell you?
3. What is being cooked in the pot?
4. Who would switch on the cooker? Why?
5. What happens when you boil an egg?
6. What is the yellow bit of the egg called?
7. Can you get thin bits of toast to dip into the yolk of the egg? Sometimes these are called 'soldiers'.
8. What happens if you boil an egg for five minutes?
9. Can you dip the toast into the yolk now?
10. Why has this happened?
11. Where do eggs come from?
12. What happens to the eggs in a bird's nest, when the mother bird sits on them to keep them warm?
13. Why should you never touch the eggs in a bird's nest?

Words beginning with *e*

Can you guess the word beginning with ***e***?

Answers: egg, eggcup, egg timer, elephant, elf, engine, elbow, envelope

Odd one out

Circle or colour in the odd one out.

Dot-to-dot elephant

Join the dots to make the shape of an elephant. Colour the elephant with lots of different colours. You can use coloured sticky paper if you have some.

THE f SOUND

(f as in fish, ph as in Phoebe)

PRONUNCIATION GUIDE

To make the **f** sound, put your top teeth onto your bottom lip, and force air through to make a *fffff*. The sound is not voiced in your throat.

LISTENING

WHAT'S ON THE CD

- The rhymes and games for the f sound include:
  - The Farmer's in his Den
  - Old Macdonald
  - Listening game

RHYMES AND SONGS

- Share rhymes and songs containing the **f** sound.

One, Two, Three, Four, Five

One, two, three, four, five,
Once I caught a fish alive,.
Six, seven, eight, nine, ten,
Then I let it go again.
Why did you let it go?
Because it bit my finger so.
Which finger did it bite?
This little finger on the right.

Old Macdonald

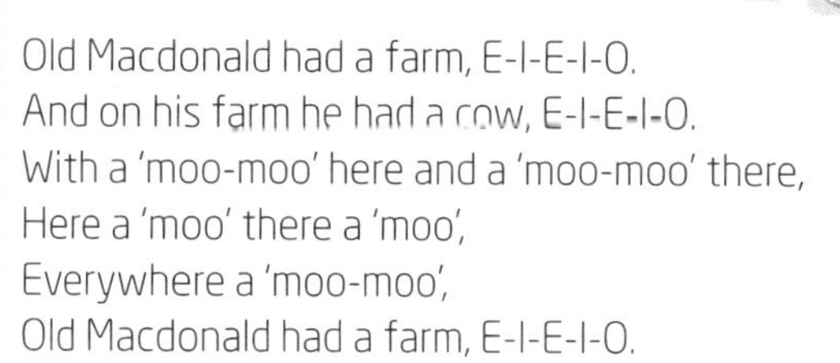

Old Macdonald had a farm, E-I-E-I-O.
And on his farm he had a cow, E-I-E-I-O.
With a 'moo-moo' here and a 'moo-moo' there,
Here a 'moo' there a 'moo',
Everywhere a 'moo-moo',
Old Macdonald had a farm, E-I-E-I-O.

Old Macdonald had a farm, E-I-E-I-O.
And on his farm he had a pig, E-I-E-I-O.
With a 'snort-snort' here and a 'snort-snort' there,
Here a 'snort' there a 'snort',
Everywhere a 'snort-snort',
With a 'moo-moo' here and a 'moo-moo' there,
Here a 'moo' there a 'moo',
Everywhere a 'moo-moo',
Old Macdonald had a farm, E-I-E-I-O.

Old Macdonald had a farm, E-I-E-I-O.
And on his farm he had a horse, E-I-E-I-O.
With a 'neigh, neigh' here and a 'neigh, neigh' there...

Little Polly Flinders

Little Polly Flinders,
Sat among the cinders,
Warming her pretty little toes.

Her mother came and caught her,
And checked her little daughter
For spoiling her nice new clothes.

The Farmer's in his Den

The farmer's in his den,
The farmer's in his den,
Ee I Enjio,
The farmer's in the den.

The farmer wants a wife,
The farmer wants a wife
Ee I Enjio,
The farmer wants a wife.

The wife wants a child...

The child wants a nurse...

The nurse wants a dog...

The dog wants a cat...

The cat wants a mouse...

The mouse wants some cheese...

We all pat the cheese.

Circle game
The farmer is in the middle of the ring and chooses a wife, and so on. At the end, the cheese is patted gently!

Five Little Pigs

Five little pigs went a-walking
(Use fingers walking.)
One little pig fell down,
One little pig ran away,
How many got into town?

Four little pigs went a-walking...

Five Little Frogs Sitting on a Well

Five little frogs sitting on a well,
(Hold up five fingers.)
One looked in and down he fell,
(Put down one finger.)
Frogs jump high, frogs jump low,
(Raise and lower fingers.)
Four little frogs dancing to and fro.
(Move four fingers.)

Four little frogs sitting on a well...
(Hold up four fingers and so on)
Three little frogs sitting on a well...
Two little frogs sitting on a well...
One little frog sitting on a well...
No little frogs sitting on a well...
(Fingers in a fist.)

ACTIVITIES

Listen to the CD and ask the children if they can guess the following sounds:
- A **frog**
- A **fire engine**
- A **flute**

■ Play an action game: an adult whispers an action to a child, remembering to emphasise the **f** sound. The child then has to act it out. Other children then try to guess the action. This is difficult, so give help and clues, so that the child is successful. For example, actions could include:
- A **fish** swimming.
- A sword **fight**.
- **Fill** a bottle or cup.
- **Float** in the water.
- **Fly** around the room.
- **Phone** a **friend**.
- **Frown**.
- **Find** something on the **floor**.
- Take a **photograph**.
- **Frighten** someone.

■ Look for story books which begin with the **f** sound and read them aloud to your class. For example:

Best Friends for Frances by Russell Hoban and Lillian Hoban (Red Fox)
Sly Fox and Red Hen (Ladybird and others)
The Princess and the Frog (Ladybird Tales)
Forgetful Little Fireman by Alan Macdonald (Ladybird Books)
A Fox Got my Socks by Hilda Offen (Red Fox)
Fifteen Ways to Go to Bed by Kathy Henderson (Frances Lincoln Children's Books)
Frog and the Stranger by Max Velthuijs (Andersen Press Ltd)
Frog Finds a Friend by Max Velthuijs (Andersen Press Ltd)

■ Look for non-fiction books in the library. You can find books about fish, farms, football and forests.
■ Find children's names beginning with the **f** sound, such as Freddy, Frank, Philip, Faisal, Fareed.
■ Ask the children to think of all the **fruits** they know. What is their **favourite**? Buy a selection of different fruits for the children to try. Make a big picture of all of the fruits. (Ensure you are aware of any food allergies before commencing this task.)

■ Ask the children to look for a **fire** extinguisher. When is it used? What would you do if you saw a fire? You could try to arrange a trip to the local fire station or look out for fire station open days.
■ Try to visit a **farm** to look at the animals there. Find out how the animals help us. For example, sheep – wool, meat; hens – eggs.
■ **Freeze** coloured water in different-sized and types of container. Smear Vaseline around the inside of the 'mould' you are using. Watch melting time for different shapes and sizes of containers.

EVALUATION

■ These questions are intended to assess the children's ability to hear the **f** sound. Ask them to rub the outside part of their ears before they start to listen.
■ Read the following questions to the children:

1. What sound is at the beginning of these words?
   fairy, face, feather, finger, fish, foot, fork, flower, fox, fruit
2. In these groups of three words, which word begins with the **f** sound?
   a) feather, dish, pig
   b) girl, boy, fairy
   c) thick, rose, fish
   d) farmer, cow, hen
   e) paper, flower, cat
   f) stamp, duck, frog
3. Clap when you hear a word with the **f** sound at the beginning:
   fish, dog, flower, feather, cat, fairy

EXTENSION ACTIVITY

■ As a further challenge for children you can try 'Robot talk'. A list of suggested words is given below.

■ The adult says the word such as 'fan' and then says it in 'Robot talk' /f/a/n/, sounding out the individual sounds. Then repeat this.

■ The child then says the word, for example 'fan'. It may take a few tries to perfect the word.

■ The adult then says the sounds and claps each one, for example /f/a/n/. Then the child joins in.

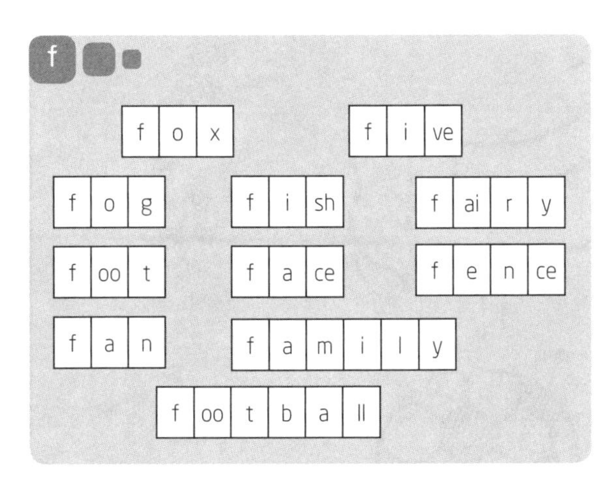

SEEING

■ Show the children photocopiable page 53 and ask them if they can identify the objects beginning with the **f** sound.

■ Make two copies of photocopiable page 53. Cut around the shapes and use them for games such as 'Snap' and 'Pairs'.

■ Show the children photocopiable page 54. Ask them to spot the five differences in the second picture.

■ Give the children photocopiable page 55 and ask them to circle or colour in all the objects that begin with the **f** sound.

THINKING

■ Ask the children to put their hands on their hips and **flap** their bent arms like a bird. Can they flap one arm, then the other, then both arms together? Ask them to run around flapping their arms.

■ Tell the children to pick up a **football**, and kick with one foot and then the other. Make a big circle on the wall. Tell them to aim the football to hit inside the circle. Encourage them to try using both feet to kick the ball.

■ Invite the children to imagine they are **fairies**, and can **fly** around the room with tiny light steps.

■ Encourage the children to imagine they are **feathers**, **floating** around the playground on the breeze.

■ Ask the children to imagine they are a **fish**. They should lie on the floor and swim around, or lie over a stool or beanbag and swim like a fish.

THINKING AND REASONING SKILLS

■ Show the children the picture on photocopiable page 52 and ask them the following questions:

1. Who is in the picture?
2. What is she doing?
3. What is the game called?
4. What is she trying to do?
5. What does she have on?
6. Who else might be there? (For example, other players, supporters).
7. What will they be doing?
8. Why do players wear a football strip?
9. Have you ever scored a goal?
10. How did you feel? Show everyone what you did.
11. Did you shout?
12. Do you support a football team?
13. What colours do they wear?
14. Why is there a lot of noise at a football match?
15. Why do people shout out?
16. When do you shout out?

Words beginning with *f*

Can you guess the word beginning with ***f***?

Answers: feather, finger, fish, foot, fork, flower, fox, fruit

Spot the difference

Can you find five things that are different in the second picture?

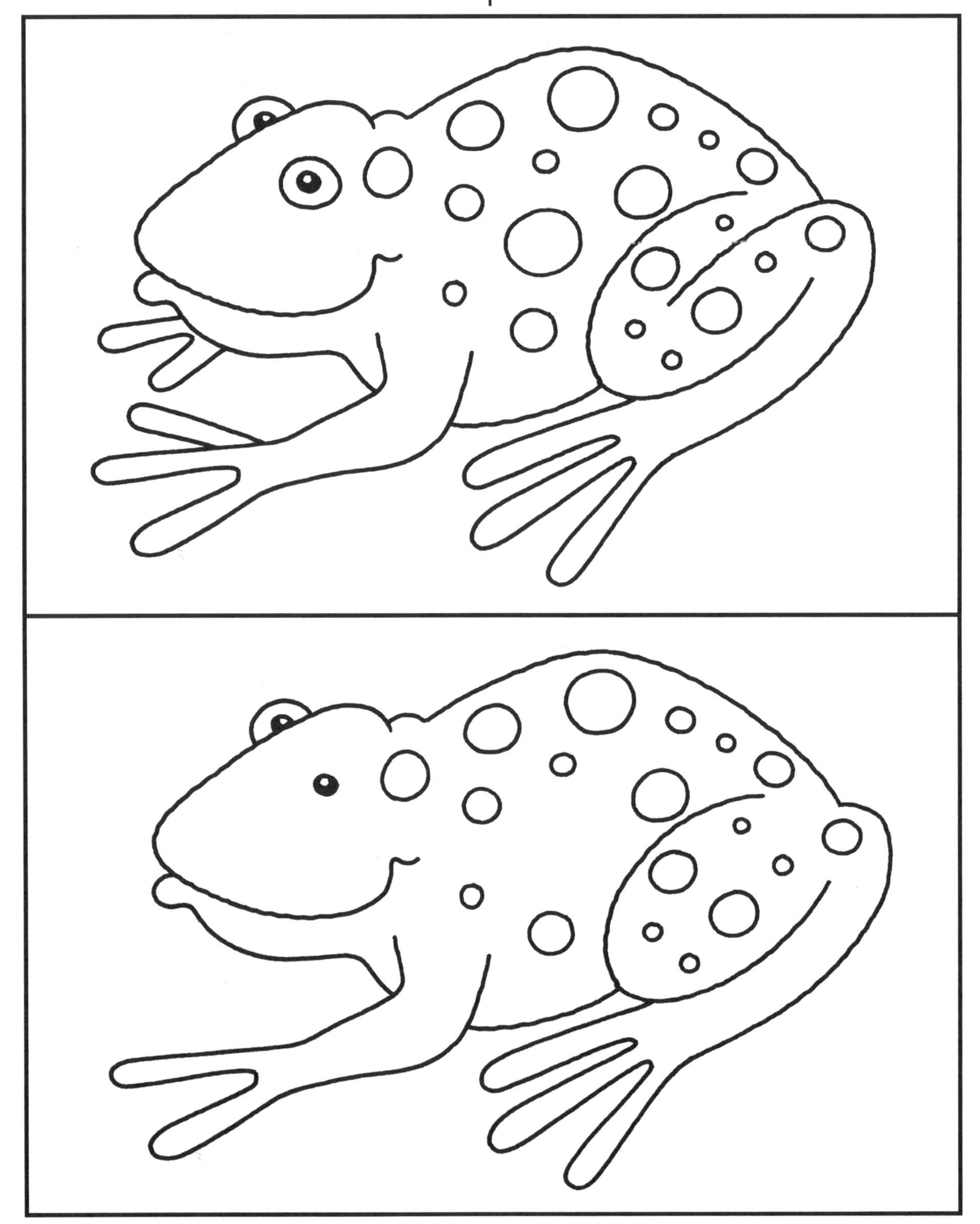

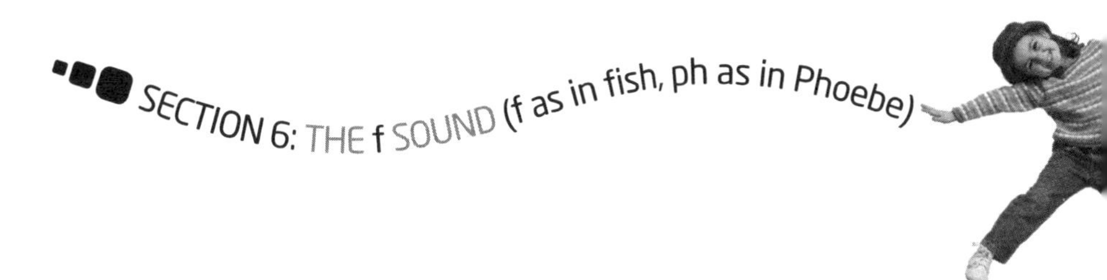

Find the *f*s

Circle or colour in the pictures that begin with the sound ***f***.

THE g SOUND

(g as in goose)

PRONUNCIATION GUIDE

The **g** sound is made at the back of the mouth. The tip of the tongue is at the back of the bottom front teeth. The sound is voiced in the throat. You can feel this like a swallowing movement.

LISTENING

WHAT'S ON THE CD

- The rhymes and games for the g sound include:
  - These are Grandma's Spectacles
  - Go to Bed, Tom
  - Goosey, Goosey, Gander
  - Listening game

RHYMES AND SONGS

- Share rhymes and songs containing the **g** sound.

Christmas is Coming

Christmas is coming, the geese are getting fat,
Please to put a penny in the old man's hat.
If you haven't got a penny, a ha'penny will do,
If you haven't got a ha'penny, then God bless you!

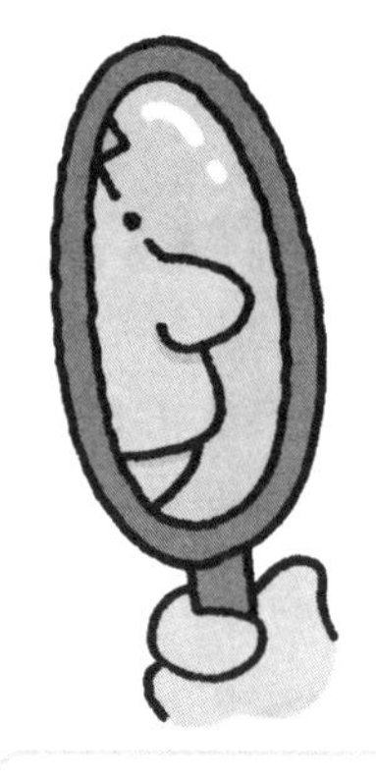

Gregory Griggs

Gregory Griggs, Gregory Griggs,
Had twenty seven different wigs.
He wore them up, he wore them down,
To please the people of the town:
He wore them east, he wore them west,
But could never tell which he liked best.

These are Grandma's Spectacles

(High voice)
These are Grandma's spectacles,
This is Grandma's hat.
This is the way she folds her hands,
And lays them in her lap.

(Deep voice)
These are grandfather's glasses,
This is grandfather's hat,
This is the way he folds his arms,
And has a little nap.

Go to Bed, Tom

Go to bed, Tom,
Go to bed, Tom,
Tired or not, Tom,
Go to bed, Tom.

Go to Bed Late

Go to bed late,
Stay very small;
Go to bed early,
Grow very tall.

Girls and Boys

Girls and boys come out to play.
The moon doth shine as bright as day.
Come with a whoop and come with a call.
Come with a good will or not at all.

Leave your supper and leave your sleep.
Come to your play fellows in the street.
Up the ladder and down the wall.
A half penny loaf will serve you all.

Goosey, Goosey, Gander

Goosey, goosey, gander
Whither shall I wander?
Upstairs and downstairs and in my lady's
chamber.
There I met an old man
Who wouldn't say his prayers,
I took him by the left leg
And threw him down the stairs.

The Grand Old Duke of York

Oh, the grand old Duke of York,
He had ten thousand men.
He marched them up to the top of the hill,
And he marched them down again.
And when they were up, they were up,
And when they were down, they were down.
And when they were only halfway up,
They were neither up nor down.

Action game

You need an even number of children, so that everyone has a partner. Six or eight is a good number. Everyone sings the verse throughout the game.

The partners line up facing each other in two equal rows. They start to sing and clap to music. The partners at the top of the line hold hands, and skip down the centre to the bottom of the rows, and back up again. As they reach their places again at the top of the row, they let go of their hands and march back (behind the other children) to the bottom of the line. When they reach the bottom of the line, they join the row again. The partners who are now at the top of the line, join hands and skip down the centre of the rows. The game continues until everyone has had a turn at dancing down the centre, and the first couple are at the top again.

SECTION 7: THE g SOUND (g as in goose)

ACTIVITIES

Listen to the CD and ask the children if they can guess the following sounds:
- A **goat**
- A **gong**
- A **guitar**

- Find some **glass** jars or bottles for the children. Together, fill the jars with different amounts of water. Gently tap the sides of the different glasses with a teaspoon. Ask the children: *Can you hear the different sounds? Can you make a tune?* Try putting sand in the jars. Can the children hear different sounds?
- Play an action game: an adult whispers an action to the child, remembering to emphasise the **g** sound. The child then has to act it out. Other children then try to guess the action. This is difficult, so give help and clues, so that the child is successful. Examples of actions could include:
  - **Giggle**.
  - Put on a **glove**.
  - Score a **goal**.
  - Be a **guard** at the castle.
  - Play the **guitar**.
- Look for story books which begin with the **g** sound and read them aloud to your class. For example:

Goldilocks and the Three Bears (Ladybird and others)
Grandfather's Pencil and the Room of Stories by Michael Foreman (Red Fox)
Going Shopping/Going to Playschool by Sarah Garland (Atlantic Monthly Press)
Green Eggs and Ham by Dr Seuss (Picture Lions)
Gorilla by Anthony Browne (Walker Books Ltd)
The Gruffalo by Julia Donaldson and Axel Scheffler (Macmillan Children's Books)
The Three Billy Goats Gruff (Ladybird and others)
Guess How Much I Love You? by Sam McBratney and Anita Jeram (Walker Books Ltd)

- Look for non-fiction books in the library. You can find books about gorillas, gardens and guinea pigs.
- Find children's names beginning with the **g** sound, such as Greg, Gordon, Gavin, Grant, Gary, Gabriel (not George or Georgia as they begin with a **j** sound).

- Use pictures from magazines and catalogues of things beginning with the **g** sound.
- Create an indoor **garden** together. Find a deep tray and put a layer of small stones at the bottom. Cover the stones with damp compost. You could grow alpine plants or herbs. Visit a garden centre to choose your plants.
- Find lots of pairs of **gloves**. Can the children match them together? Match them by colour, size or pattern. Ask: *What different kinds of gloves can you buy?* (For example: oven, gardening, boxing, woollen, cloth, leather, fingerless.)

EVALUATION

- These questions are intended to assess children's ability to hear the **g** sound. Ask them to rub the outside part of their ears before they start to listen.
- Read the following questions to the children:
  1. What sound is at the beginning of these words?
     goose, gorilla, glove, grass, goldfish, garden
  2. In these groups of three words, which word begins with the **g** sound?
     a) gate, house, plant
     b) night, cook, guitar
     c) horse, garden, sea
     d) glove, bread, wash
     e) book, sand, gorilla
     f) bone, goat, bird
  3. Clap when you hear a word with a **g** sound at the beginning:
     wool, goldfish, gorilla, spoon, giggle, gate, trampoline, girl

EXTENSION ACTIVITY

■ As a further challenge for children you can try 'Robot talk'. A list of suggested words is given below.

■ The adult says the word such as 'gap' and then says it in 'Robot talk' /g/a/p/, sounding out the individual sounds. Then repeat this.

■ The child then says the word, for example 'gap'. It may take a few tried to perfect the word.

■ The adult then says the sounds and claps each one, for example /g/a/p/. Then the child joins in.

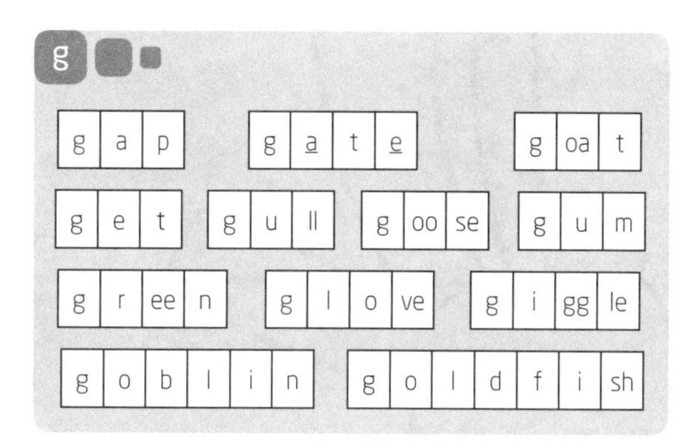

SEEING

■ Show the children photocopiable page 61 and ask them if they can identify the objects beginning with the **g** sound

■ Make two copies of photocopiable page 61. Cut around the shapes and use them for games such as 'Snap' and 'Pairs'.

■ Display photocopiable page 62. Can the children spot the five differences in the second picture?

■ Show the children photocopiable page 63. Ask them to point to the pictures of goldfish.

THINKING

■ Play a **game** with a ball on the **grass**. Ask the children to try to kick the ball with one foot, then the other foot. Let them jump on a patch of grass and then jump on concrete. Does it feel the same? Why/why not?

■ Tell the children to imagine they are musicians in a rock band. Encourage them to strum on their **guitars** as they dance to the music.

■ Ask the children to imagine they are the world's biggest **gorilla**: walking around beating their chests, taking great strong steps, pretending to climb up a tree. Tell them to imagine they have a bunch of bananas, peeling back the skins and eating them. Can they make a gorilla noise?

■ Encourage the children to dig in an imaginary **garden**. They can then pretend to plant some plants or sow seeds.

■ Invite the children to imagine they are a **goldfish** swimming in a bowl. Encourage them to lie on the floor and make swimming movements. Look at the people outside the goldfish bowl. Are they making faces?

■ Pretend you are all going to a pet shop to see a **guinea** pig. Ask the children to imagine holding the little animal in their hands, and stroking the soft, shiny fur. Ask: *How does this make you feel? Have you got a real pet?*

THINKING AND REASONING SKILLS

■ Show the children the picture on photocopiable page 60 and ask them the following questions:

1. Where is this happening?
2. What animal is in the picture?
3. What do rabbits like to eat?
4. How many rabbits are in the picture?
5. Where do rabbits live?
6. Do gardeners like rabbits in their garden? Why?/why not?
7. Do farmers like rabbits in their fields? Why?/why not?
8. Have you seen a pet rabbit?
9. Where does a pet rabbit live?
10. Do you know what a pet rabbit eats?
11. Can you find out?
12. Draw a picture of the rabbit you would like to have. Is it a boy or a girl rabbit?
13. What name would it have? Close your eyes, and imagine stroking the rabbit.

Words beginning with *g*

Can you guess the word beginning with ***g***?

Answers: girl, glove, guitar, goldfish, goat, grape, glass, goose

Spot the difference

Can you find five things that are different in the second picture?

Find the goldfish

Point to the pictures of the goldfish.

THE h SOUND

(h as in house)

PRONUNCIATION GUIDE
To make the **h** sound, open your mouth a little, and push out the air.

LISTENING

WHAT'S ON THE CD

- The rhymes and games for the h sound include:
  - Hot Cross Buns!
  - Humpty Dumpty
  - A Hunting We Will Go
  - Listening game

RHYMES AND SONGS

- Share rhymes and songs containing the **h** sound.

Clap your hands

Clap your hands, clap your hands
Clap them just like me.
Comb your hair, comb your hair,
Comb it just like me
Touch your shoulders, touch your shoulders
Touch them just like me.
Tap your knees, tap your knees,
Tap them just like me.
Shake your head, shake your head,
Shake it just like me.
Clap your hands, clap your hands
Then let them quiet be.

Hickory, Dickory, Dock

Hickory, dickory, dock
The mouse ran up the clock.
(Run your fingers up your arm.)
The clock struck one,
(Clap once.)
The mouse ran down,
(Run your fingers down your arm again.)
Hickory, dickory, dock.

Horsey, Horsey

Horsey, horsey, don't you stop,
Just let your feet go clippetty-clop;
Your tail goes swish, and the wheels go round –
Giddy up, we're homeward bound.

Horsey, horsey, don't delay,
Just let your feet run any old way,
Your tail goes swish, and the wheels go round –
Giddy up, we're homeward bound.

Actions
Use coconut shells to make the sound of a horse's hooves. Make the horse move slowly (trot), then go fast (gallop). Shout 'giddy up, horsey', as you gallop along!

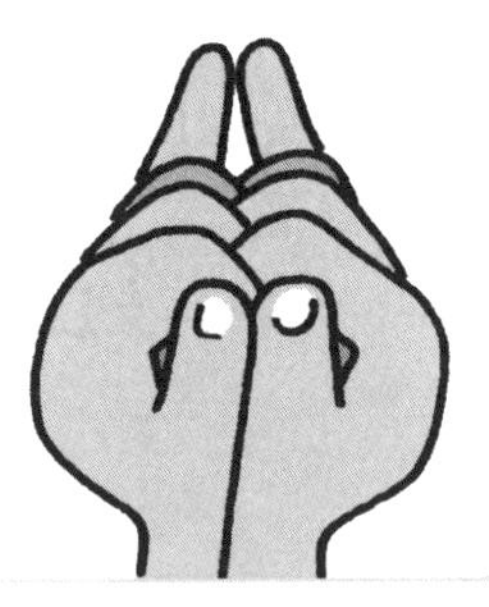

Here is the Church

Here is the church.
(Clasp your hands together, with fingers facing inwards.)
Here is the steeple.
(Make a tower shape with your index fingers.)
Open the doors,
(Open the thumbs.)
And see all the people.
(Turn hands inside out and wiggle all the fingers.)

Hot Cross Buns!

Hot cross buns! Hot cross buns!
One a penny, two a penny
Hot cross buns!
If your daughters do not like them
Give them to your sons;
One a penny, two a penny
Hot cross buns!

Humpty Dumpty

Humpty Dumpty sat on a wall,
Humpty Dumpty had a great fall.
All the king's horses,
And all the king's men
Couldn't put Humpty together again.

A Hunting We Will Go

A hunting we will go, a hunting we will go,
We'll catch a fox and put him in a box,
And then we'll let him go!

A hunting we will go, a hunting we will go,
We'll catch a fish and put him on a dish,
And then we'll let him go!

A hunting we will go, a hunting we will go,
We'll catch a bear and cut his hair,
And then we'll let him go!

A hunting we will go, a hunting we will go,
We'll catch a pig and dance a little jig,
And then we'll let him go!

A hunting we will go, a hunting we will go,
We'll catch a giraffe and make him laugh,
And then we'll let him go!

Circle game

Form a circle, with the children holding hands. Choose one child to stand outside the circle. This child is going to be the 'fox'.

Tell the children in the circle to dance to the right, while the 'fox' dances around the outside of the circle, to the left.

On the line 'We'll catch...' the two children nearest the 'fox' form an arch and let the 'fox' into the middle of the circle.

On the line 'we'll let him go!' the children let him go and the 'fox' chooses a new child to be the 'fox'.

SECTION 8: THE h SOUND (h as in house)

ACTIVITIES

Listen to the CD and ask the children if they can guess the following sounds:
- A **hen**
- A **horse**
- A **harp**
- A **heart** beating

■ Play an action game: an adult whispers an action to the child, remembering to emphasise the **h** sound. The child then has to act it out. Other children try to guess the action. This is difficult, so give help and clues, so that the child is successful. Here are some examples of actions:
- **Hop** up and down.
- **Hold** something in your **hand**.
- Use a **hammer**.
- Be **happy**.
- **Hide**.
- Cluck like a **hen**.
- Touch your **head**.
- Touch your **hair**.
- Point to your **heart**.

■ Look for story books which begin with the **h** sound and read them aloud to your class. For example:

The Happy Hedgehog Band by Martin Waddell and Jill Barton (Candlewick Press)
Hairy Maclary from Donaldson's Dairy by Lynley Dodd (Viking Children's Books)
Hairy Maclary, Sit by Lynley Dodd (Spindlewood)
Harold and the Purple Crayon by Crockett Johnson (Non Basic Stock Line)
Handa's Surprise by Eileen Browne (Walker Books Ltd)
A House is a House for Me by Mary Ann Hoberman and Betty Fraser (Puffin Books)

■ Look for non-fiction books in the library about horses, hamsters, hedgehogs, houses and hospitals.
■ Find children's names beginning with the **h** sound, such asHamish, Henry, Harvey, Heidi, Hadeel.
■ Ask the children to draw a large house shape and fill it with pictures from magazines and catalogues of things beginning with the **h** sound.
■ Ask the children if they have tasted **hummus.** The recipe is easy and it is delicious in sandwiches or as a dip for vegetables. You need: one can of chickpeas,

one clove of garlic, three tablespoons of lemon juice, four tablespoons of Tahini (sesame seed paste). Drain half the liquid out of the can of chickpeas. Put all the ingredients into a food mixer and mix on high, stirring occasionally until it is a creamy paste. (Make sure you are aware of any food allergies before commencing this activity.)
■ Find out about the Jewish festival of **Hanukkah**.

EVALUATION

■ These questions are intended to assess children's ability to hear the **h** sound. Ask them to rub the outside part of their ears before they start to listen.
■ Read the following questions to the children:

1. What sound is at the beginning of these words?
   hand, hammer, hamster, handbag, hat, head, hedgehog, hen, horse, hair
2. In these groups of three words, which word begins with the **h** sound?
   a) home, bear, tiger
   b) bag, road, hippopotamus
   c) coat, head, swan
   d) hamster, car, turnip
   e) face, song, hen
   f) heart, fork, knife
3. Clap when you hear a word with the **h** sound at the beginning:
   horse, bag, hill, heat, hedgehog, song, holiday, holly, mouse, house

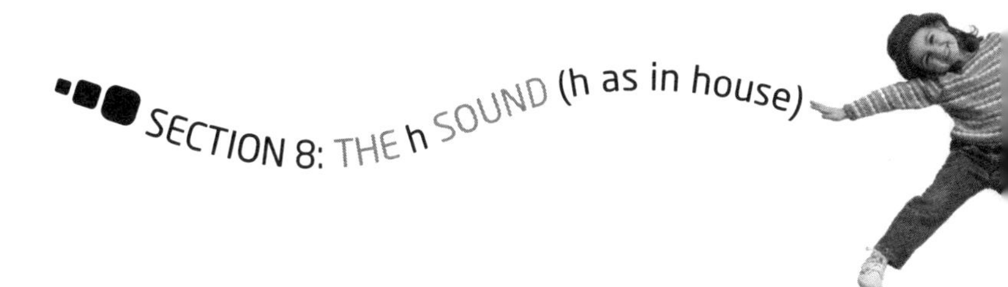

EXTENSION ACTIVITY

■ As a further challenge for children you can try 'Robot talk'. A list of suggested words is given below.

■ The adult says the word such as 'hat' and then says it in 'Robot talk' /h/a/t/, sounding out the individual sounds. Then repeat this.

■ The child then says the word, for example 'hat'. It may take a few tries to perfect the word.

■ The adult then says the sounds and claps each one, for example /h/a/t/. Then the child joins in.

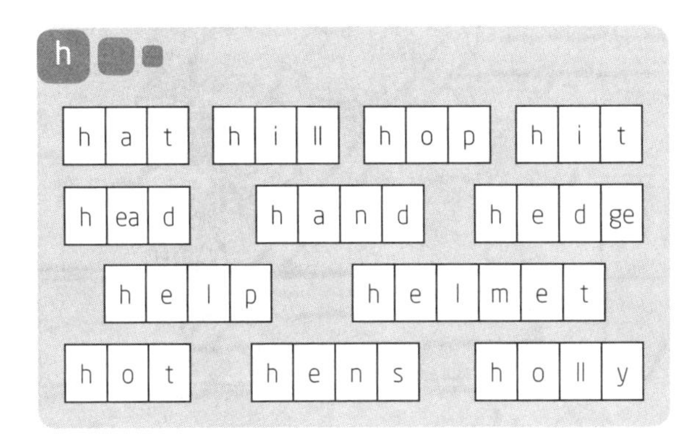

SEEING

■ Show the children photocopiable page 69. Ask them if they can identify the objects beginning with the **h** sound.

■ Make two copies of photocopiable page 69. Cut around the shapes and use them for games such as 'Snap' and 'Pairs'.

■ Display photocopiable page 70. Ask the children to match the shadow in each line to its object.

■ Hand out copies of photocopiable page 71. Encourage the children to point to the odd one out in each row.

THINKING

■ Ask the children to **hop** on one leg, then on the other leg. Try small hops, then big hops.

■ Teach the children to play **hopscotch**. Draw a suitable grid in the playground outside. Encourage the children to try hopping with one foot and then with the other. There are lots of websites showing different ways to play hopscotch.

■ Throw a ball or a beanbag into a **hoop**. Tell the children to use one **hand**, then use the other. Remind them to keep watching the ball or beanbag all the time.

■ Teach the children to do bunny **hops** on a mat.

■ Ask the children to imagine they are in a **horse** race. Tell them:

You have a beautiful white horse, and you are feeling very ***happy****. Put the saddle onto your horse, and get up on his back. Ride around and try to win the race. If you touch anyone else, you have lost the race.*

You win! Let everyone see how happy you are! Take off the horse's saddle. Brush the horse with a hand brush. Give the horse a feed of oats and a drink of water.

■ Tell the children to imagine they are going on a **holiday**. Ask them: *Where would you like to go? Is it sunny or cold? What will you pack into your suitcase? Who will go with you? What games will you play? Will you be sad to come home again?*

THINKING AND REASONING SKILLS

■ Show the children the picture on photocopiable page 68 and ask them the following questions:

1. What is happening in the picture?
2. How many hens are in the hen house?
3. What are they eating?
4. What do hens lay?
5. What will the hens do when they see the open door?
6. Who left the door open?
7. What will the farmer do?
8. Will the hens be in any danger? Why?
9. What noise does a cockerel make?
10. When does he make this noise?
11. How does the person who left the door open, feel about the mistake?
12. How would you feel?
13. What would you say to the farmer?
14. What would he say to you?

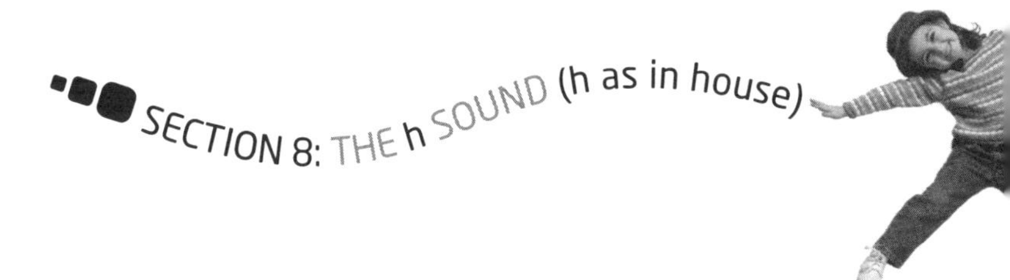

Words beginning with *h*

Can you guess the word beginning with ***h***?

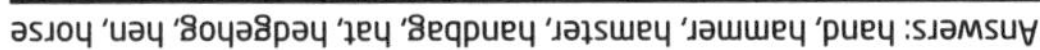

Match the shadow

Match the picture to its shadow.

Odd one out

Point to the odd one out.

THE i SOUND

(i as in insect)

PRONUNCIATION GUIDE

To make the sound **i**, open your mouth partially, and pull back the sides of your mouth slightly. The sound is made at the back of the throat.

LISTENING

WHAT'S ON THE CD

- The rhymes and games for the **i** sound include:
  - If You're Happy and You Know It
  - In and Out the Dusty Bluebells
  - Listening game

RHYMES AND SONGS

- Share rhymes and songs containing the **i** sound.

Incy Wincy Spider

Incy wincy spider
Climbing up the spout;
Down came the rain
And washed the spider out:
Out came the sun
And dried up all the rain;
Incy wincy spider
Climbing up again.

It's Raining, it's Pouring

It's raining, it's pouring;
The old man is snoring.
He went to bed
And bumped his head
And he couldn't get up in the morning.

If You're Happy and You Know It

If you're happy and you know it,
Clap your hands,
If you're happy and you know it,
Clap your hands,
If you're happy and you know it,
And you really want to show it,
If you're happy and you know it,
Clap your hands.

If you're happy and you know it,
Stamp your feet...

If you're happy and you know it,
Shake your arms...

If you're happy and you know it,
Nod your head...

If you're happy and you know it,
Turn around...

If you're happy and you know it,
Bounce up and down...

If you're happy and you know it,
Scream and shout...

Christmas is Coming

Christmas is coming, the geese are getting fat,
Please to put a penny in the old man's hat.
If you haven't got a penny, a ha'penny will do,
If you haven't got a ha'penny, then God bless you!

If All the World Were Paper

If all the world were paper,
And all the sea were ink,
If all the trees were bread and cheese,
What should we do for drink?

In and Out the Dusty Bluebells

In and out the dusty bluebells,
In and out the dusty bluebells,
In and out the dusty bluebells,
I am your master.

Pitterpitter patter on your shoulder,
Pitterpitter patter on your shoulder,
Pitterpitter patter on your shoulder,
I am your master.

Actions

Children form a ring, with hands joined and raised to form arches. One child (the master) skips in and out of the raised hands, and stops at the nearest child, when the line 'I am your master' is sung. The master taps on the shoulder of that child while everyone sings 'Pitterpitter patter'. The child holds the master by the waist, and follows him or her, weaving in and out the raised arms. This goes on until there are no children in the circle, and everyone is following the master.

Noise

Billy is blowing his trumpet;
Bertie is banging a tin;
Betty is crying for Mummy,
And Bob has pricked Ben with a pin.
Baby is crying out loudly;
He's out on the lawn with his pram.
I am the only one silent
And I've eaten all the jam.

If You Should Meet a Crocodile

If you should meet a crocodile,
Don't take a stick and poke him;
Ignore the welcome in his smile,
Be careful not to stroke him.
For as he sleeps upon the Nile,
He thinner gets and thinner;
But whene'er you meet a crocodile
He's ready for his dinner.

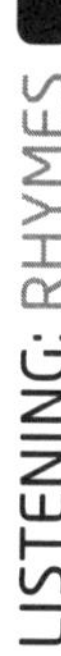

ACTIVITIES

Listen to the CD and ask the children if they can guess the missing words in the sentences. The sentences and answers are below.
- A flute, a violin, a drum and harp are all types of... (**instrument**)
- An ant, a bee and a fly are all types of... (**insect**)
- My pen is filled with... (**ink**)

- Ask the children: *Can you make the sounds of an* ***insect*** *buzzing around?*
- Discuss musical **instruments**. Can the children recognise the sounds when they cannot see which instrument is being played? Play a game: ask a child to hide so that they cannot be seen by the rest of the class. Ask them to play a simple musical instrument. Can the other children guess what instrument is being played?
- Play an action game: an adult whispers an action to the child, remembering to emphasise the **i** sound. The child then has to act it out. Other children then try to guess the action. This is difficult, so give help and clues, so that the child is successful. For example, actions could be:
  - Play a musical **instrument**.
  - Be an **insect**.
  - **Invite** a friend to play.
  - Be **ill**.
  - Scratch an **itch**.
- Look for story books which begin with the **i** sound and read them aloud to your class. For example:

Imagine by Alison Lester (Allen & Unwin)
Inside Mary Elizabeth's House by Pamela Allen (Puffin Books)
If You Give a Mouse a Cookie by Laura Joffe Numeroff and Felicia Bond (HarperPaperbacks)

- Look for non-fiction books in the library. You can find books about insects, igloos and Indian foods.
- Find children's names beginning with the **i** sound, such as Innes, Irving, Imraan, Idan, Ilan, India, Ingrid, Isabel, Imogen, Inaaya, Ilana.
- Display all the musical **instruments** that you can find. Do the children know the names of the instruments?
- Ask the children to make a list of all the **insects** they know. Find a reference book in the library to help them with this.

- Take a large piece of paper outdoors. Drop tiny drops of **ink** on the paper. Ask the children if they can make pretty patterns. Use different colours.

EVALUATION

- These questions are intended to assess children's ability to hear the **i** sound. Ask them to rub the outside part of their ears before they start to listen.
- Read the following questions to the children:
  1. What sound is at the beginning of these words?
     insect, instrument, igloo, Indian, itch, invitation, ink, infant
  2. In each group of three words, which word begins with the **i** sound?
     a) ink, face, run
     b) gate, invitation, spider
     c) cake, insect, toad
     d) inside, ant, cook
     e) horse, dog, infant
     f) lamb, chicken, igloo
  3. Clap when you hear a word with an **i** sound at the beginning:
     chicken, igloo, insect, lamb, indoors, robber, itch

EXTENSION ACTIVITY

- As a further challenge for children you can try 'Robot talk'. A list of suggested words is given below.
  - The adult says the word such as 'ink' and then says it in 'Robot talk' /i/n/k/, sounding out the individual sounds. Then repeat this.
  - The child then says the word, for example 'ink'. It

may take a few tries to perfect the word.

■ The adult then says the sounds and claps each one, for example /i/n/k/. Then the child joins in.

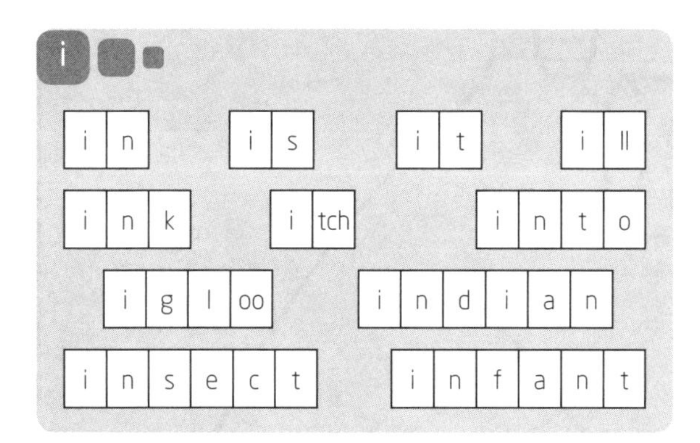

SEEING

■ Show the children photocopiable page 77. Ask them if they can identify the objects beginning with the **i** sound.

■ Make two copies of photocopiable page 77. Cut around the shapes and use them for games such as 'Snap' and 'Pairs'.

■ Ask the children to find the five differences in the second picture on photocopiable page 78.

■ Display photocopiable page 79. Invite the children to help the Inuit find his way home to his igloo, by tracing the path either with a finger or a pencil. Encourage them to move their eyes from left to right as they complete the activity.

THINKING

■ Go for a walk to the park or into the garden together. How many **insects** can the children find? Do not pick them up, just watch them moving around. Find out their names. Ask the children to pretend they are insects, crawling around looking for food.

■ Tell the children to **imagine** they are in an orchestra. Encourage them to play all the musical **instruments** they can think of. Ask: *What is your favourite instrument? Can you be the conductor of the orchestra?* Encourage them to make big shapes with their hands and arms. Play marching music and conduct the orchestra.

■ Encourage the children to imagine they are an **Inuit inside** their house, called an **igloo**. It is very cold, and they must put on special clothes to keep warm. Ask: *What clothes will you put on?* Tell them to put them on, one by one, and then pretend to go outside to throw snowballs with each of their hands.

■ Imagine the class receive an **invitation** to a party. Ask: *Who is having the party? What will you wear? What would you like to eat? What games are you going to play?*

THINKING AND REASONING SKILLS?

■ Show the children the picture on photocopiable page 76 and ask them the following questions:

1. Who is in the picture?
2. What is he doing?
3. Why is he in bed?
4. What is wrong with the boy?
5. Has the doctor come to see him?
6. What did the doctor say?
7. How long has he got to stay in bed?
8. Have you been ill in bed?
9. What was wrong with you?
10. How does it feel to be ill?
11. How does it feel to be better?

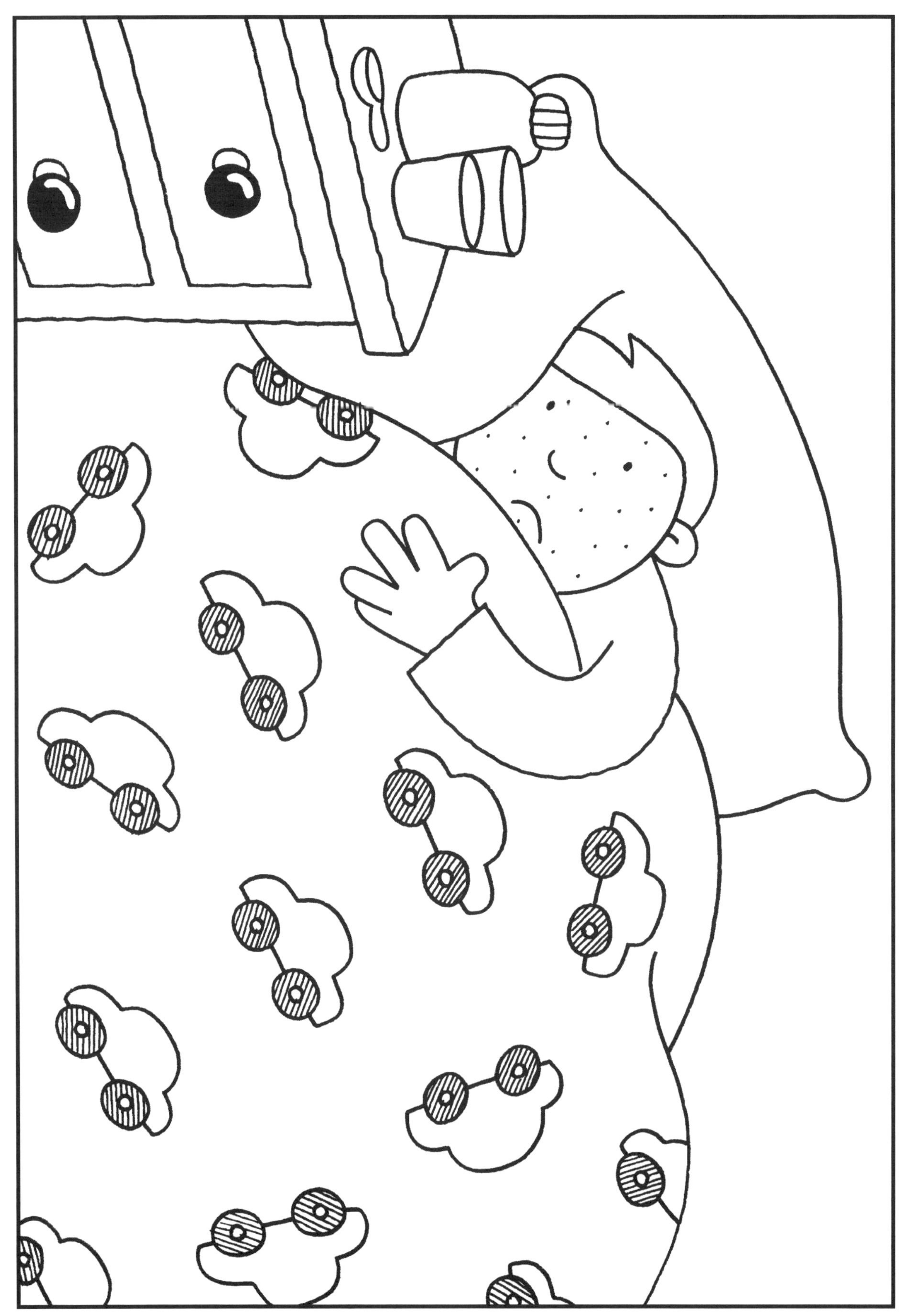

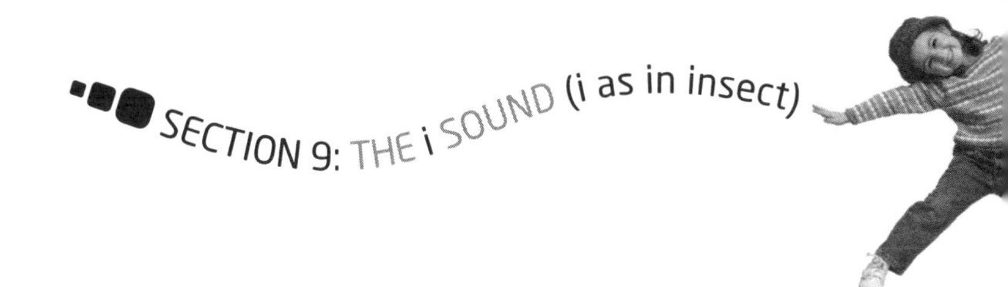

Words beginning with *i*

Can you guess the word beginning with ***i***?

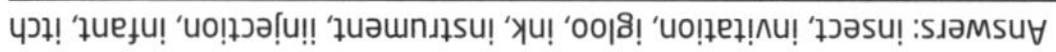

Spot the difference

Can you find five things that are different in the second picture?

Help the Inuit

Help the Inuit to reach his igloo through the snowy mountains.

THE j SOUND

(j as in jelly, g as in George)

PRONUNCIATION GUIDE

To make the **j** sound, stick your lips out slightly. Your tongue is near the top of your mouth and it moves when you open your mouth. The **j** sound is made by using the voice. You can feel the movement in the throat.

LISTENING

WHAT'S ON THE CD

- The rhymes and games for the j sound include:
  - Jack Be Nimble
  - Jack and Jill
  - Listening game

RHYMES AND SONGS

- Share rhymes and songs containing the **j** sound.

Jack Sprat

Jack Sprat could eat no fat.
His wife could eat no lean.
And so betwixt the two of them,
They licked the platter clean.

Jack ate all the lean,
Joan ate all the fat.
The bone they picked it clean,
Then gave it to the cat.

Jack Be Nimble

Jack be nimble, Jack be quick,
Jack jump over the candlestick.

Jack and Jill

Jack and Jill went up the hill
To fetch a pail of water;
Jack fell down and broke his crown,
And Jill came tumbling after.
Up got Jack, and home did trot,
As fast as he could caper.
He went to bed and bound his head,
With vinegar and brown paper.

Georgie Porgie

Georgie Porgie, pudding and pie,
Kissed the girls and made them cry;
When the boys came out to play,
Georgie Porgie ran away.

Little Jumping Joan

Here am I,
Little jumping Joan;
When nobody's with me
I'm all alone!

Jack-in-the-box

Jack-in-the-box jumps up like this,
He makes me laugh, when he waggles his head.
I gently push him down again,
Saying 'Jack-in-the-box, you must go to bed.'

This is the House that Jack Built

This is the house that Jack built.

This is the malt
That lay in the house that Jack built.

This is the cat
That ate the malt
That lay in the house that Jack built.

This is the cat,
That killed the rat,
That ate the malt
That lay in the house that Jack built.

This is the dog,
That worried the cat,
That killed the rat,
That ate the malt
That lay in the house that Jack built.

This is the cow with the crumpled horn,
That tossed the dog,
That worried the cat,
That killed the rat,
That ate the malt
That lay in the house that Jack built.

This is the maiden all forlorn,
That milked the cow with the crumpled horn,
That tossed the dog,
That worried the cat,
That killed the rat,
That ate the malt
That lay in the house that Jack built.

This is the man all tattered and torn,
That kissed the maiden all forlorn,
That milked the cow with the crumpled horn,
That tossed the dog,
That worried the cat,
That killed the rat,
That ate the malt
That lay in the house that Jack built.

This is the priest all shaven and shorn,
That married the man all tattered and torn,
That kissed the maiden all forlorn,
That milked the cow with the crumpled horn,
That tossed the dog,
That worried the cat,
That killed the rat,
That ate the malt
That lay in the house that Jack built.

This is the cock that crowed in the morn,
That waked the priest all shaven and shorn,
That married the man all tattered and torn,
That kissed the maiden all forlorn,
That milked the cow with the crumpled horn,
That tossed the dog,
That worried the cat,
That killed the rat,
That ate the malt
That lay in the house that Jack built.

This is the farmer sowing the corn,
That kept the the cock that crowed in the morn,
That waked the priest all shaven and shorn,
That married the man all tattered and torn,
That kissed the maiden all forlorn,
That milked the cow with the crumpled horn,
That tossed the dog,
That worried the cat,
That killed the rat,
That ate the malt
That lay in the house that Jack built.

ACTIVITIES

Listen to the CD and ask the children if they can guess the missing words in the sentences. The sentences and answers are below.
- When it is cold outside, I like to wear a big, warm... (**jumper**)
- My favourite pudding is ice cream and ... (**jelly**)
- At lunchtimes I eat sandwiches and drink orange... (**juice**)
- Monkeys, snakes and tigers all live in the... (**jungle**)

- Play an action game: an adult whispers an action to the child, remembering to emphasise the **j** sound. The child then has to act it out. Other children then try to guess the action. This is difficult, so give help and clues, so that the child is successful. For example, actions could include:
  - **Jump** up and down.
  - Do a **judo** move.
  - Tell a **joke**.
  - **Jog** on the spot.
  - **Jingle** coins or bells.
  - Drink **juice**.
- Look for story books which begin with the **j** sound and read them aloud to your class. For example:

Just like Jasper! by Nick Butterworth and Mark Inkpen (Hodder Children's Books)
Jack's Fantastic Voyage by Michael Foreman (Harcourt)
Jack's Big Race by Michael Foreman (Andersen Press Ltd)
Jamela's Dress by Niki Daly (Frances Lincoln Children's Books)
Jack and the Beanstalk (Ladybird and others)
The Giraffe who Got in a Knot by John Bush and Paul Geraghty (Red Fox)
Jungle Book (Disney Classics) by Rudyard Kipling

- Look for non-fiction books in the library. You can find books about jellyfish, jewels, jumping games.
- Find children's names beginning with the **j** sound, such as James, John, Jack, George, Jalaal, Joel, Gemma, Georgia, Judith, Jade, Joyce, Jadeeda, Jasra.
- Use pictures from magazines and catalogues of things beginning with the **j** sound. Find pictures of **jewels**. How many colours of **gem** stones can you find?
- Ask the children if they have ever watched someone making a **jelly**. What flavour do they like best? Ask: *Do you like jelly beans? What is your favourite colour?*
- Ask the children if they like **jam**. Look for all the jam flavours you can buy. Ask: *Do you have a favourite? Do you like jammy dodger biscuits or jam tarts?* Make jam sandwiches with the children. Use different cutters to make shapes. (Make sure you are aware of any food allergies before commencing this activity.)

EVALUATION

- These questions are intended to assess children's ability to hear the **j** sound. Ask them to rub the outside part of their ears before they start to listen.
- Read the following questions to the children:

1. What sound is at the beginning of these words?
   jam, jelly, jellyfish, jigsaw, jumper, jar, Jack-in-the-box, jelly beans, jacket, jug
2. In each group of three words, which word begins with the **j** sound?
   a) jelly, sand, big
   b) ham, ran, jam
   c) up, jug, garden
   d) jumper, hook, animal
   e) yellow, dog, jacket
   f) June, pot, circle
3. Clap when you hear a word with a **j** sound at the beginning:
   January, February, March, April, May, June, July, August, September, October, November, December

LISTENING: NOTES

EXTENSION ACTIVITY

■ As a further challenge for children you can try 'Robot talk'. A list of suggested words is given below.

■ The adult says the word such as 'jam' and then says it in 'Robot talk' /j/a/m/, sounding out the individual sounds. Then repeat this.

■ The child then says the word, for example 'jam'. It may take a few tries to perfect the word.

■ The adult then says the sounds and claps each one, for example /j/a/m/. Then the child joins in.

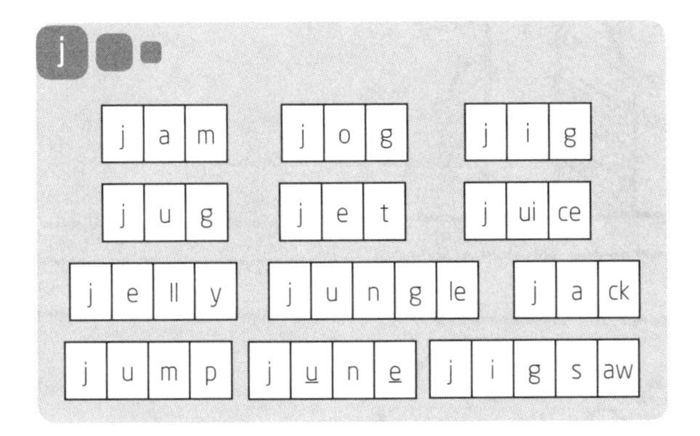

SEEING

■ Show the children photocopiable page 85 and ask them if they can identify the objects beginning with the **j** sound.

■ Make two copies of photocopiable page 85. Cut around the shapes and use them for games such as 'Snap' and 'Pairs'.

■ Display photocopiable page 86. Ask the children if they can find the five differences in the second picture on the sheet.

■ Hand out copies of photocopiable page 87 to the children. Ask them to circle or colour in the objects that begin with the **j** sound.

THINKING

■ Ask the children to **jump** up and down like a **Jack-in-the-box**: they should curl up very small, then jump up to reach the sky, shouting 'hello' as they do so. Then they should curl up into their box again.

■ Invite the children to **jog** around the playground. How many times can they jog around before getting tired? Try this on different days, counting the laps. See if the children can make a new record every day.

■ Find a piece of rope. Can the children **jump** over the rope? Ask two children to hold each end of the rope and show them how to turn it round and round. Can a third child jump into the rope? Teach the children some songs to sing when jumping in and out of the rope.

■ Encourage the children to imagine they are a shaking, shivering **jelly**. Tell them to walk around, shaking all over like a wobbly jelly.

■ Tell the children to imagine they have a great big heavy **jug** of **juice** and two cups. Imagine that they are pouring juice into one cup and then the other cup. Pretend to put the jug into their other hand. Is it harder to pour with one hand than the other?

■ Ask the children to imagine they are getting dressed. They need to put on their **jeans**, **jumper**, **jacket** and **jewels**.

■ Invite the children to imagine they are in a **jungle**. Ask: *What animals might be there? Can you be a monkey and **jump** from tree to tree?*

■ Have the children heard the story '**Jack** and the Beanstalk'? Ask them to imagine they are Jack, climbing up the beanstalk. When they get to the top, they walk to the **giant's** castle. They pick up a sword and fight the giant for the magic hen, then take the hen back home to their mum.

THINKING AND REASONING SKILLS

■ Show the children the picture on photocopiable page 84 and ask them the following questions:

1. Who is in the picture?
2. What has she made?
3. What shape is the jelly bowl?
4. Is the jelly liquid or solid in the picture?
5. Why is it going into the fridge?
6. How will you know when it is ready to eat?
7. What flavour is it?
8. What is your favourite flavour?
9. How often do you eat jelly in a week?
10. What do you like to eat with jelly?

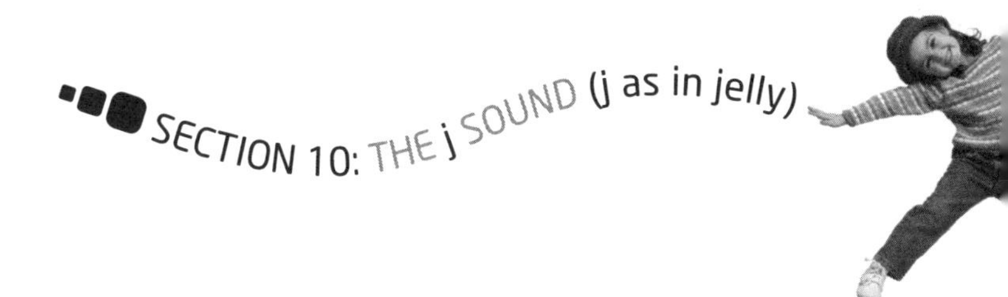

Words beginning with *j*

Can you guess the word beginning with ***j***?

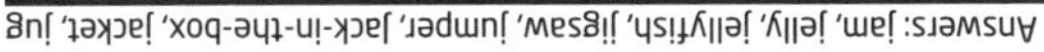
Answers: jam, jelly, jellyfish, jigsaw, jumper, jack-in-the-box, jacket, jug

Spot the difference

Can you find five things that are different in the second picture?

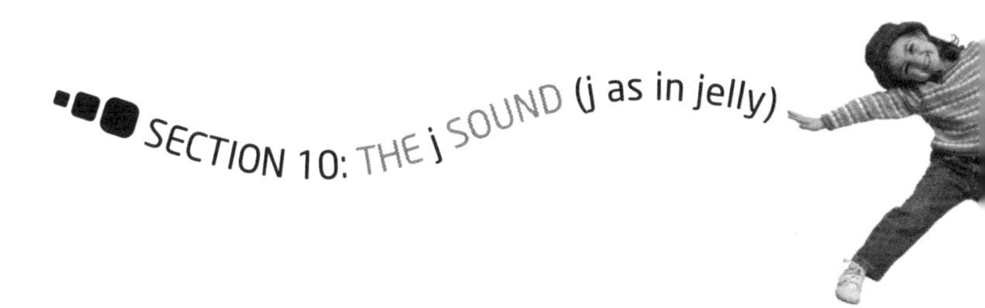

Find the *j*s

Circle or colour in the pictures that begin with the sound ***j***.

THE l SOUND
(l as in lorry)

PRONUNCIATION GUIDE
To make the l sound, move your tongue to the roof of your mouth behind your teeth. The tongue stays at the front of the mouth while the sound is made at the back of the mouth.

LISTENING

WHAT'S ON THE CD
- The rhymes and games for the l sound include:
  - Lavender's Blue
  - Here We Go Looby Loo
  - Listening game

RHYMES AND SONGS
- Share rhymes and songs containing the l sound.

Lavender's Blue

Lavender's blue, diddle, diddle,
Lavender's green.
When I am king, diddle, diddle,
You shall be queen.

Call up your men, diddle, diddle,
Set them to work.
Some to the plough, diddle, diddle,
Some to the cart.

Some to make hay, diddle, diddle,
Some to thresh corn.
Whilst you and I, diddle, diddle,
Keep ourselves warm.

Here We Go Looby Loo

Here we go looby loo,
Here we go looby lye,
Here we go looby loo,
All on a Saturday night.

You put your right hand in,
You take your right hand out,
You shake it a little, a little,
And turn yourself about.

Here we go looby loo...

You put your left foot in,
You take your left foot out,
You shake it a little, a little,
And turn yourself about.

Here we go looby loo...

You put your right foot in...

Here we go looby loo...

You put your whole self in...

Here we go looby loo...

Lucy Locket

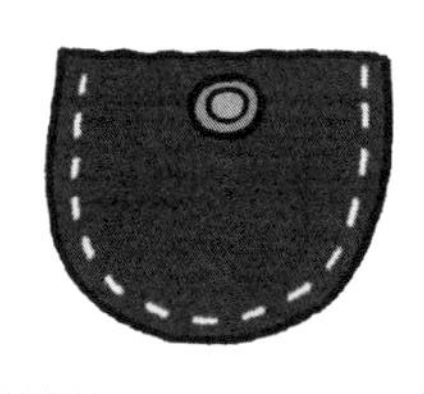

Lucy Locket lost her pocket,
Kitty Fisher found it;
Not a penny was there in it
Only ribbon round it.

London Bridge is Falling Down

London Bridge is falling down,
Falling down, falling down,
London Bridge is falling down,
My fair lady.

Build it up with iron bars,
Iron bars, iron bars,
Build it up with iron bars,
My fair lady.

Iron bars will bend and break,
Bend and break, bend and break,
Iron bars will bend and break,
My fair lady.

Build it up with gold and silver,
Gold and silver, gold and silver,
Build it up with gold and silver,
My fair lady.

I Sent a Letter to My Love

I sent a letter to my love,
And on the way, I dropped it,
One of you picked it up
And put it in your pocket.

Circle game

Play the game 'I Sent a Letter to My Love' (or the handkerchief game) with the children. Everyone sits or stands in a circle, holding hands. One child skips around the outside of the circle, and has a letter (or handkerchief) in his/her hand. Everyone sings the song.

When the children sing the last line of the song, the child with the letter should drop it behind one of the children in the circle, who should immediately pick it up. The two children run in opposite directions around the circle to get back to the empty space. The last one to get back becomes IT.

Ladybird, Ladybird

Ladybird, ladybird, fly away home,
Your house is on fire and your children all gone,
All except one and that's little Ann,
For she has crept under the warming pan.

Mary Had a Little Lamb

Mary had a little lamb
Its fleece was white as snow;
And everywhere that Mary went,
The lamb was sure to go.

It followed her to school one day,
That was against the rule;
It made the children laugh and play,
To see a lamb at school.

And so the teacher turned it out,
But still it lingered near,
And waited patiently about
Till Mary did appear.

'Why does the lamb love Mary so?'
The eager children cry;
'Why, Mary loves the lamb, you know,'
The teacher did reply.

ACTIVITIES

Listen to the CD and ask the children if they can guess the missing words in the sentences. The sentences and answers are below.
- On hot summer days I like to drink fizzy... (**lemonade**)
- I like sitting on the beach and eating ice... (**lollies**)
- What am I? I am an insect. I am very tiny. I have red wings with black spots on them. (a **ladybird**)

- Play an action game: an adult whispers an action to the child, remembering to emphasise the **l** sound. The child then has to act it out. Other children then try to guess the action. This is difficult, so give help and clues, so that the child is successful. For example, actions could include:
  - **Listen** to a sound.
  - **Lose** something.
  - **Lift** something heavy.
  - **Laugh**.
  - **Lock** the door.
  - Put on the **light**.
  - **Lead** the way.
  - Eat a **lemon**.
  - **Lick** a **lollipop**.
- Look for story books which begin with the **l** sound and read them aloud to your class. For example:

The Bad-tempered Ladybird by Eric Carle (Puffin Books)
Chicken Licken (Ladybird Tales and others)
The Lighthouse Keeper's Lunch by Ronda Armitage and David Armitage (Scholastic Children's Books)
The Lighthouse Keeper's Rescue by David Armitage and Ronda Armitage (Scholastic Children's Books)
There was an Old Lady who Swallowed a Fly by Pam Adams (Child's Play International Ltd)
Little Hotchpotch by Brian Patten and Mike Terry (Bloomsbury Publishing)
Little Beaver and the Echo by Amy McDonald and Sarah Fox-Davies (Walker Books Ltd)

- Look for non-fiction books in the library. You can find books about leaves, lobsters, lizards and lions.
- Find children's names beginning with the **l** sound, such as Luke, Lewis, Liam, Lesley, Louise, Lily.
- Use pictures from magazines and catalogues of things beginning with the **l** sound – for example, lamps, lights, lanterns and ladders.
- When you are out a walk in summer together, look for **ladybirds** on the **leaves**. Ladybirds are usually red with black spots. Ask the children to find a picture of a ladybird in the **library**.
- Ask the children if they have tasted **lemon** curd, lemon jelly or lemon meringue pie.
- Try an Indian drink called **lassi**. It is a sweetened yoghurt drink. It is delicious with your favourite fruit **liquidised** in it.
- Ask the children to **look** around for **litter lying** on the ground. Find out where the litter bins are in your street/area. Tell the children that they must never drop litter.

EVALUATION

- These questions are intended to assess the children's ability to hear the **l** sound. Ask them to rub the outside part of their ears before they start to listen.
- Read the following questions to the children:
  1. What sound is at the beginning of these words?
     lamb, light, lemonade, lion, leg, laugh, lizard
  2. In these groups of three words, which word begins with the **l** sound?
     a) lion, ape, food
     b) jam, money, lamp
     c) child, lamb, car
     d) hand, penny, lollipop
     e) ladder, monkey, hen
     f) bring, sand, lemonade
  3. Clap when you hear a word with the **l** sound at the beginning:
     lamp, lion, head, ladder, lizard, jump, lettuce

EXTENSION ACTIVITY

■ As a further challenge for children you can try 'Robot talk'. A list of suggested words is given below.

■ The adult says the word such as 'lip' and then says it in 'Robot talk' /l/i/p/, sounding out the individual sounds. Then repeat this.

■ The child then says the word, for example 'lip'. It may take a few tries to perfect the word.

■ The adult then says the sounds and claps each one, for example /l/i/p/. Then the child joins in.

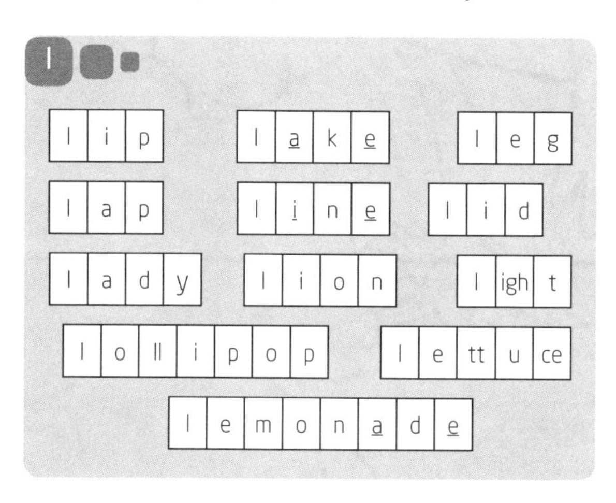

SEEING

■ Show the children photocopiable page 93 and ask them if they can identify the objects beginning with the **l** sound.

■ Make two copies of photocopiable page 93. Cut around the shapes and use them for games such as 'Snap' and 'Pairs'.

■ Ask the children to find the five differences in the second picture on photocopiable page 94.

■ Provide the children with copies of photocopiable page 95. Ask them to join up the pairs of matching lollipops, either by tracing with a finger or drawing a pencil line.

■ Encourage the children to climb the **ladder** at the chute or slide in the playground, using their arms and **legs** to climb.

■ Ask the children to hop on one leg, and then on the other. Find or make a straight **line** on the ground. Can the children hop down the line without falling over? Now try hopping down the line on the other leg. Encourage the children to use their arms to help them balance.

■ Draw a set of **ladders** on the ground. Ask the children to jump between the bars. How far can they jump? Can they jump two or more spaces on the ladder?

■ Invite the children to imagine they are a **lion** in the jungle. Tell them to roar as **loudly** as they can. Then try a **little** quiet roar before doing a great loud roar again. Tell them to roam about in the jungle, crawling on their hands and knees. They should shake their manes, roaring so that everyone knows they are there.

■ Ask the children to imagine they are a **lizard**, sliding about on their tummy – poking out their **long** tongue, **looking** for flies to eat. They should pretend to catch a fly, swallow it, and then slide around looking for more.

■ Encourage the children to imagine that they have a bottle of **lemonade**. Ask them to pour some (imaginary) lemonade carefully into cups for their friends. They should take the cups of lemonade to their friends, watching that they do not spill a single drop. This is a pretend tea-party. What other things can the children pretend to eat?

THINKING AND REASONING SKILLS

■ Show the children the picture on photocopiable page 92 and ask them the following questions:

1. Who is in the picture?
2. What is the mummy doing?
3. Why is the mummy looking at the label?
4. What does a label tell you on a jumper?
5. What different sorts of jumpers can you get?
6. What sort of jumper would you like? Can you design one?
7. Have you all chosen the same colour and pattern?
8. Why do we not all like the same things?

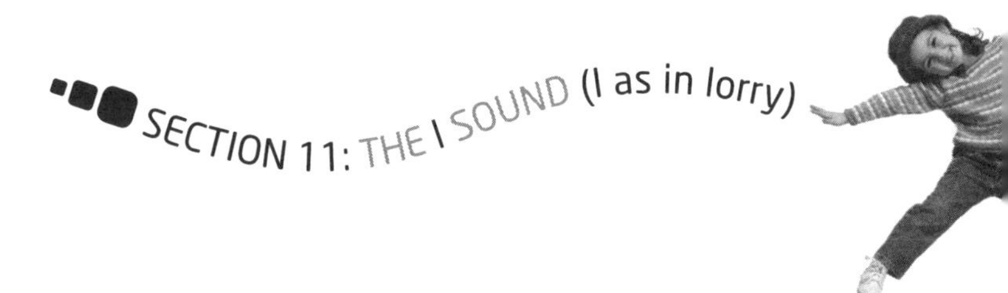

Words beginning with *l*

Can you guess the word beginning with ***l***?

Answers: lion, lamb, lips, lollipop, lemon, ladybird, lamp, leaf

Spot the difference

Can you find five things that are different in the second picture?

Match the lollipops

Join up the lollipops that are the same shape.

THE m SOUND

(m as in mouse)

PRONUNCIATION GUIDE
To make the **m** sound, press your lips together and then make the sound down your nose.

LISTENING

WHAT'S ON THE CD

- The rhymes and games for the m sound include:
  - Have You Seen the Muffin Man?
  - Here We Go Round the Mulberry Bush
  - Listening game

RHYMES AND SONGS

- Share rhymes and songs containing the **m** sound.

Mary, Mary, Quite Contrary

Mary, Mary, quite contrary,
How does your garden grow?
With silver bells and cockle shells,
And pretty maids all in a row.

Ten Little Men

Ten little men standing straight,
(Ten fingers held up.)
Ten little men open the gate,
(Push hands apart.)
Ten little men all in a ring,
(Make a ring with fingers.)
Ten little men bow to the king,
(Bend fingers.)
Ten little men dance all day,
(Make fingers dance.)
Ten little men hide away.
(Put hands behind back.)

Have You Seen the Muffin Man?

Have you seen the muffin man?
The muffin man, the muffin man,
Oh, have you seen the muffin man,
Who lives in Drury Lane?

Oh yes, I've seen the muffin man,
The muffin man, the muffin man,
Oh yes, I've seen the muffin man,
Who lives in Drury Lane.

Moses Toes-es

Moses supposes his toes-es are roses,
But Moses supposes erroneously.
For nobody's toes-es are posies of rosies,
As Moses supposes his toes-es to be.

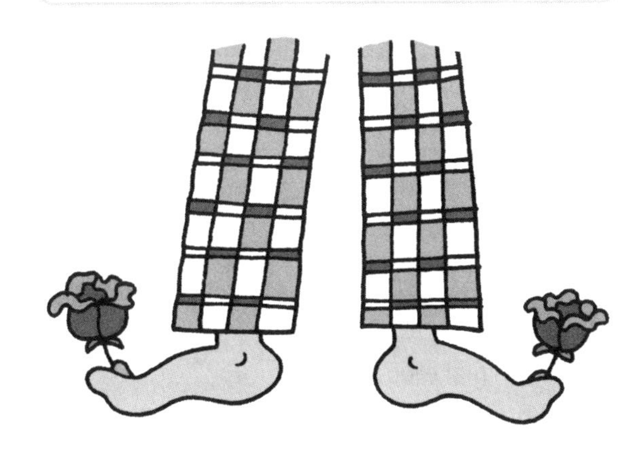

Mousie Comes A-creeping, Creeping

Mousie comes a-creeping, creeping.
Mousie comes a-peeping, peeping.
Mousie says, 'I'd like to stay,
But I haven't got the time today.'
Mousie popped into his hole,
And said 'Achoo!
I've caught a cold!'

Little Miss Muffet

Little Miss Muffet
Sat on a tuffet,
Eating her curds and whey;
There came a big spider,
Who sat down beside her
And frightened Miss Muffet away.

Here We Go Round the Mulberry Bush

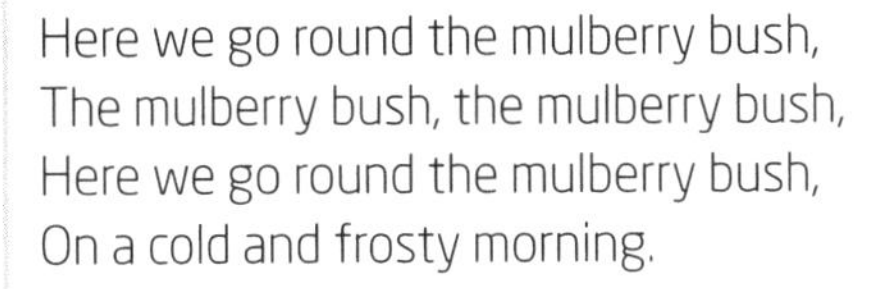

Here we go round the mulberry bush,
The mulberry bush, the mulberry bush,
Here we go round the mulberry bush,
On a cold and frosty morning.

This is the way we wash our hands,
Wash our hands, wash our hands,
This is the way we wash our hands
On a cold and frosty morning.

Here we go round the mulberry bush...

This is the way we wash our face...

This is the way we clean our teeth...

This is the way we brush our hair...

This is the way we put on our clothes...

Circle game
Children join hands to form a circle and dance around during the chorus. During the verses they perform the relevant action (for example, they pretend to wash their hands).

ACTIVITIES

Listen to the CD and ask the children if they can guess the following sounds:
- A **mouse**
- A **motorbike**
- A **monster**

■ Play an action game: an adult whispers an action to the child, remembering to emphasise the **m** sound. The child then has to act it out. Other children then try to guess the action. This is difficult, so give help and clues, so that the child is successful. For example, actions could include:
- **March** up and down.
- **Mend** a hole in your clothes.
- Put on **make-up**.
- **Munch** a biscuit.
- **Mop** the floor.

■ Look for story books which begin with the **m** sound and read them aloud to your class. For example:

Meg and Mog Stories by Helen Nicoll and Jan Pienkowski (Puffin Books)
The Little Mermaid by Hans Christian Andersen (Dover Publications)
The Book about Moomin, Mymble and Little My by Tove Jansson and Sophie Hannah (Sort Of Books UK)
The Mousehole Cat by Antonia Barber and Nicola Bayley (Walker Books Ltd)
Mister Magnolia by Quentin Blake (Red Fox)

■ Look for non-fiction books in the library. You can find books about cows and milk, mountains, moths, making masks, and the moon.
■ Find children's names beginning with the **m** sound, such as Mark, Matthew, Michael, Mohammed, Margaret, Mollie, Melissa, Muna, Meir.
■ Use pictures from magazines and catalogues of things beginning with the **m** sound.
■ Give the children **magnets**. Ask them to walk around their environment trying to lift things with them. Ask them the following questions: *What does the magnet lift up? Do you have fridge magnets in your house? Why do they stick on the fridge?*
■ Ask the children if they can find **milk**, **mushrooms**, **melons**, **mustard**, **meat**, **marmalade** in the shops. Find out all the foods you can make from milk and if possible try them (for example, cheese, yoghurt, curds, cream, butter). (Make sure you are aware of any of allergies before doing this.)

■ Grow **mung** bean sprouts and eat them.

EVALUATION

■ These questions are intended to assess the children's ability to hear the **m** sound. Ask them to rub the outside part of their ears before they start to listen.
■ Read the following questions to the children:

1. What sound is at the beginning of these words?
man, mend, mop, melon, mud, marmalade, money, mitten

2. In these groups of three words, which word begins with the **m** sound?
- **a)** mummy, cat, bird
- **b)** ban, can, man
- **c)** head, moon, beach
- **d)** mermaid, pig, house
- **e)** hill, down, monkey
- **f)** rattle, leg, mirror

3. Clap when you hear a word with the **m** sound at the beginning:
mother, map, mitten, dog, milk, magic, mountain, lip, market

EXTENSION ACTIVITY

■ As a further challenge for children you can try 'Robot talk'. A list of suggested words is given below.
- The adult says the word such as 'mat' and then says it in 'Robot talk' /m/a/t/, sounding out the individual sounds. Then repeat this.
- The child then says the word, for example 'mat'.

It may take a few tries to perfect the word.

■ The adult then says the sounds and claps each one, for example /m/a/t/. Then the child joins in.

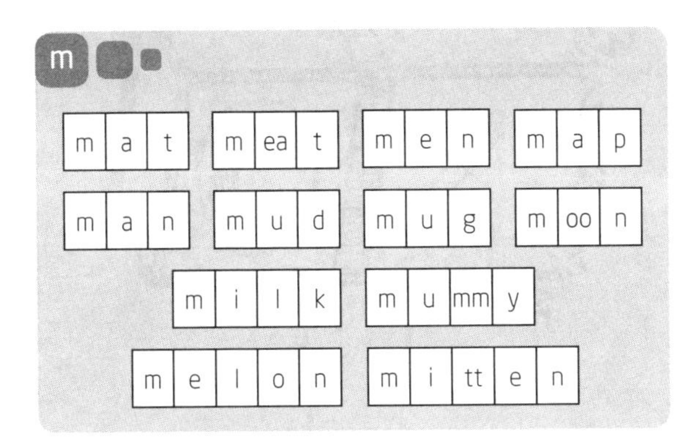

SEEING

■ Show the children photocopiable page 101 and ask them if they can identify the objects beginning with the **m** sound.

■ Make two copies of photocopiable page 101. Cut around the shapes and use them for games such as 'Snap' and 'Pairs'.

■ Display photocopiable page 102. Can the children tell you which is the correct missing piece of the puzzle?

■ Show the children photocopiable page 103. Ask them to help the monkey to follow the pathway to reach his bananas. They can do this by tracing with a finger, or drawing a line with a pencil. Encourage them to move their eyes from left to right as they complete the activity.

THINKING

■ Ask the children to **march** around like a soldier, swinging their arms at their sides. Ask: *How quickly can you march?* Tell them to make their legs do big steps – heads in the air, backs straight. If available, play some marching **music** and ask the children to march in time to it.

■ Encourage the children to imagine they are a **mouse**. Can they squeak? Ask them to **move** about like a mouse on their hands and knees. They should move slowly at first, then quickly: waggling their long tail, sitting up on their two back legs and sniffing around for cheese to eat. Ask: *Do you like being a mouse? Why/why not?*

■ Ask the children to imagine they are a **monkey**, climbing up trees, making monkey noises and peeling bananas to eat. Encourage them to scamper around on their hands and feet like a monkey.

■ Tell the children to imagine they are on a **motorbike**. Make a noise like a motorbike. Move around fast without touching another motorbike or having a crash. Show them how to lean to one side when they turn a corner.

THINKING AND REASONING SKILLS

■ Show the children the picture on photocopiable page 100 and ask them the following questions:

1. What has happened in the picture?
2. What does the man have on his head? Why?
3. What else is he wearing?
4. Why did he fall off his motorbike?
5. What would you do, if you were there?
6. Who would you phone?
7. What is the phone number for an ambulance and the police?
8. Where was the man going?
9. What do you wear to go out on a bicycle?
10. Have you had an accident on your bicycle?
11. What happened?
12. Who was with you?
13. What did they do?
14. Do you have stabilisers on your bike? Draw a picture of a bicycle or a tricycle you would like to own.

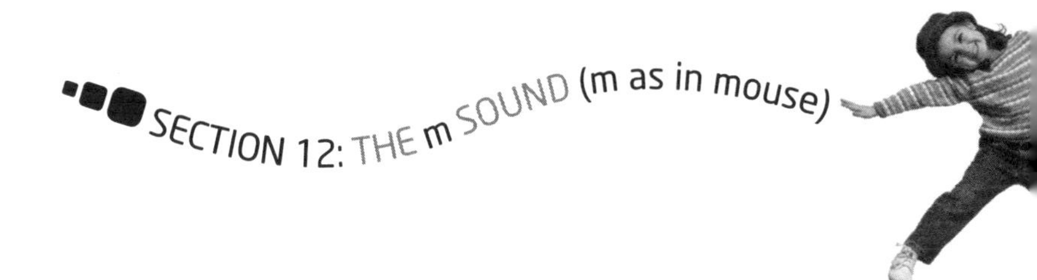

Words beginning with *m*

Can you guess the word beginning with ***m***?

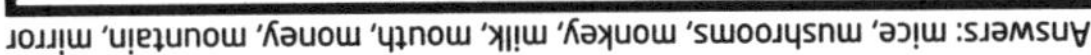

Matching game

Can you match the missing piece in the jigsaw?

Help the monkey

Help the monkey to reach the bananas, through the jungle paths.

THE n SOUND

(n as in nest and kn as in knee)

PRONUNCIATION GUIDE

To make the **n** sound, the tip of the tongue goes behind the top teeth and the tongue does not move. The sound is made in the nose.

LISTENING

WHAT'S ON THE CD

- The rhymes and games for the n sound include:
  - This Old Man, He Played One
  - Listening game

RHYMES AND SONGS

- Share rhymes and songs containing the **n** sound.

I Had a Little Nut Tree

I had a little nut tree,
Nothing would it bear
But a silver nutmeg
And a golden pear;
The King of Spain's daughter
Came to visit me,
And all for the sake
Of my little nut tree.

Nuts in May

Here we come gathering nuts in May
Nuts in May, nuts in May
Here we come gathering nuts in May
On a cold and frosty morning.

Knees Up Mother Brown

There came a girl from France,
Who didn't know how to dance.
The only thing that she could do
Was knees up Mother Brown.

Oh, knees up Mother Brown,
Knees up Mother Brown,
Knees up, knees up, never let the breeze up,
Knees up Mother Brown.

Oh, hopping on one foot,
Hopping on one foot,
Hopping, hopping, never stopping,
Hopping on one foot.

Oh, knees up Mother Brown...

Oh, prancing up and down,
Prancing up and down,
Prancing, prancing, never dancing,
Prancing up and down.

Oh, knees up Mother Brown...

And whirling round and round,
Whirling round and round,
Whirling, whirling, never twirling,
Whirling round and round.

Oh, knees up Mother Brown...

This Old Man, He Played One

This old man, he played one,
He played knick-knack on my thumb,
With a knick-knack, paddywhack,
Give a dog a bone;
This old man came rolling home.

This old man, he played two,
He played knick-knack on my shoe...

This old man, he played three,
He played knick-knack on my knee...

This old man, he played four,
He played knick-knack at my door...

This old man, he played five,
He played knick-knack on my hive...

This old man, he played six,
He played knick-knack on my sticks...

This old man, he played seven,
He played knick-knack up in heaven...

This old man, he played eight,
He played knick-knack on my gate...

This old man, he played nine,
He played knick-knack on my spine...

This old man, he played ten,
He played knick-knack once again...

I'm a Nut

I'm an acorn, small and round,
Lying on the cold, cold ground.
Everyone walks over me,
That is why I'm cracked you see.

I'm a nut!
(*Click, click with your tongue.*)
I'm a nut!
(*Click, click with your tongue.*)
I'm a nut!
(*Click, click with your tongue.*)

My Grandfather's Clock

My grandfather's clock
Was too large for the shelf,
So it stood ninety years on the floor;
It was taller by half
Than the old man himself,
Though it weighed not a pennyweight more.

It was bought on the morn
Of the day that he was born,
And was always his treasure and pride;
But it stopped, short,
Never to go again,
When the old man died.

Ninety years without slumbering,
Tick, tock, tick, tock,
His life seconds numbering,
Tick, tock, tick, tock,
It stopped, short,
Never to go again,
When the old man died.

SECTION 13: THE n SOUND (n as in nest)

ACTIVITIES

Listen to the CD and ask the children if they can guess what the sound effects are.
- What is the person blowing? (**nose**)
- What is the person doing to the door? (**knocking**)
- What is the horse doing? (**neighing**)

■ Play an action game: an adult whispers an action to the child, remembering to emphasise the **n** sound. The child then has to act it out. Other children then try to guess the action. This is difficult, so give help and clues, so that the child is successful. For example, actions could include:
- **Nod** your head.
- **Notice** something.
- Sew with a **needle**.
- Read a **newspaper**.
- Touch your **neck**.
- Touch your **nose**.
- Shake your head (**no**).

■ Look for story books which begin with the **n** sound and read them aloud to your class. For example:

Noisy Nora by Rosemary Wells (Puffin Books)
Not Now, Bernard by David McKee (Red Fox)
Don't Put Your Finger in the Jelly, Nelly by Nick Sharratt (Scholastic Children's Books)
The Giraffe who Got in a Knot by John Bush and Paul Geraghty (Red Fox)
Nini at the Carnival by Errol Lloyd (Red Fox)

■ Look for non-fiction books in the library. You can find books about bird nests, newspapers, nurses and names.

■ Find children's names beginning with the **n** sound, such as Norman, Nicholas, Nigel, Nicole, Nancy, Nadine, Natasha, Nada, Naomi.

■ Ask the children what **numbers** they know. For those who are better with numbers, try this trick. Ask: *How many fingers do you have?* When the children answer 'ten' say: *No you don't. You have eleven. Let me show you.* With one hand, count down, touching the fingers 10, 9, 8, 7, 6. Then say: *The other hand has five fingers, so six add on five makes eleven. You have eleven fingers.*

■ Ask the children to look for objects beginning with the **n** sound in the cupboard and in the

supermarket. Look for **nectarines** and different types of **nuts**.

■ You can make a game called **ninepin** bowling. Collect **nine** empty plastic drinks bottles, all the same size, and fill them with dry sand. Find a tennis ball, or a larger ball or beanbag. Put all the bottles together in a diamond formation. Move back from them and make a line to stand on. The children roll the ball hard to knock down the 'pins', or throw the beanbag. Count out the **number** that have fallen.

EVALUATION

■ These questions are intended to assess children's ability to hear the **n** sound. Ask them to rub the outside part of their ears before they start to listen.

■ Read the following questions to the children:

1. What sound is at the beginning of these words?
   nest, nose, nut, nurse, neck, number, noise
2. In these groups of three words, which word begins with the **n** sound?
   a) nut, robber, box
   b) fog, fry, number
   c) arrow, needle, cut
   d) men, nurse, monkey
   e) net, fish, catch
   f) straw, drink, nest
3. Clap when you hear a word with the **n** sound at the beginning:
   bird, nest, number, necklace, ring, nose, neck

EXTENSION ACTIVITY

■ As a further challenge for children you can try 'Robot talk'. A list of suggested words is given below.

■ The adult says the word such as 'nut' and then says it in 'Robot talk' /n/u/t/, sounding out the individual sounds. Then repeat this.

■ The child then says the word, for example 'nut'. It may take a few tries to perfect the word.

■ The adult then says the sounds and claps each one, for example /n/u/t/. Then the child joins in.

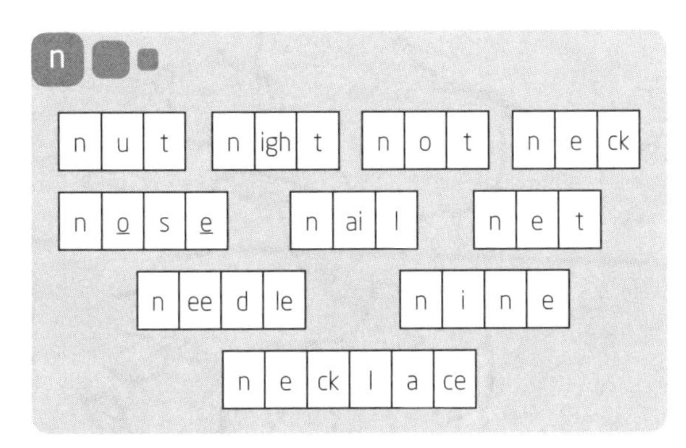

SEEING

■ Show the children photocopiable page 109 and ask them if they can identify the objects beginning with the **n** sound.

■ Make two copies of photocopiable page 109. Cut around the shapes and use them for games such as 'Snap' and 'Pairs'.

■ Show the children photocopiable page 110. Can they find the five differences in the second picture on the sheet?

■ Display photocopiable page 111. Ask the children to point to the odd one out in each row.

THINKING

■ Ask the children to pretend they are hammering a nail into a piece of wood, first with one hand and then with the other.

■ Ask the children to take big breaths in through their **noses** and out through their mouths. They could lie on the ground, sit on a chair or stand. Tell them to put their hands on their tummies. Then take a big breath in through their nose, and push out their tummy. Then let the breath out slowly through their mouth. Try this three times. Encourage the children to do this when they are angry or upset. Explain that it helps to make people feel calm again.

■ Smelling game: collect together some things for the children to smell with their **noses**. Blindfold them and ask them to guess what the smell is. Good smells to use are oranges, perfume, cheese, vinegar, coffee, lemon. (Be aware that being blindfolded is very upsetting for some children.)

■ Play football with a soft ball. Ask the children to kick the balls into a **net**. Tell them to try with their right leg, then with their left.

THINKING AND REASONING SKILLS

■ Show the children the picture on photocopiable page 108 and ask them the following questions:

1. What animal is in the picture?
2. What is it collecting?
3. What colour can a squirrel be?
4. Why is the squirrel collecting nuts?
5. What time of year is it?
6. What does a squirrel do with the nuts?
7. What do you call the long sleep that some animals have in winter?
8. Do we hibernate in winter?
9. Do we have to save up food for the winter?
10. Where do you buy your food?
11. Can you buy food all year round?

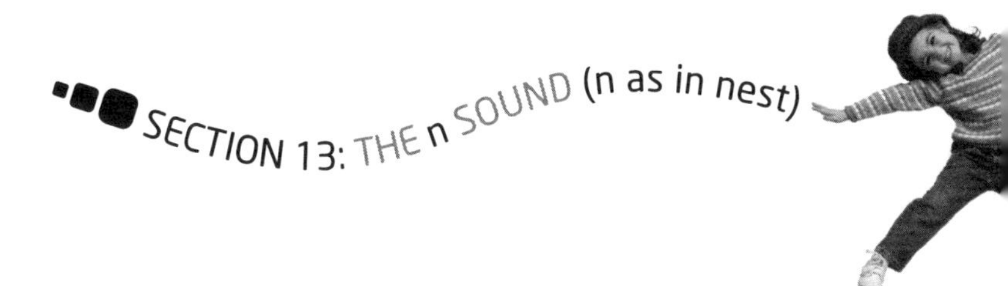

Words beginning with *n*

Can you guess the word beginning with ***n***?

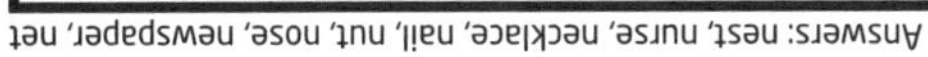
Answers: nest, nurse, necklace, nail, nut, nose, newspaper, net

Spot the difference

Can you find five things that are different in the second picture?

Odd one out

Point to the odd one out.

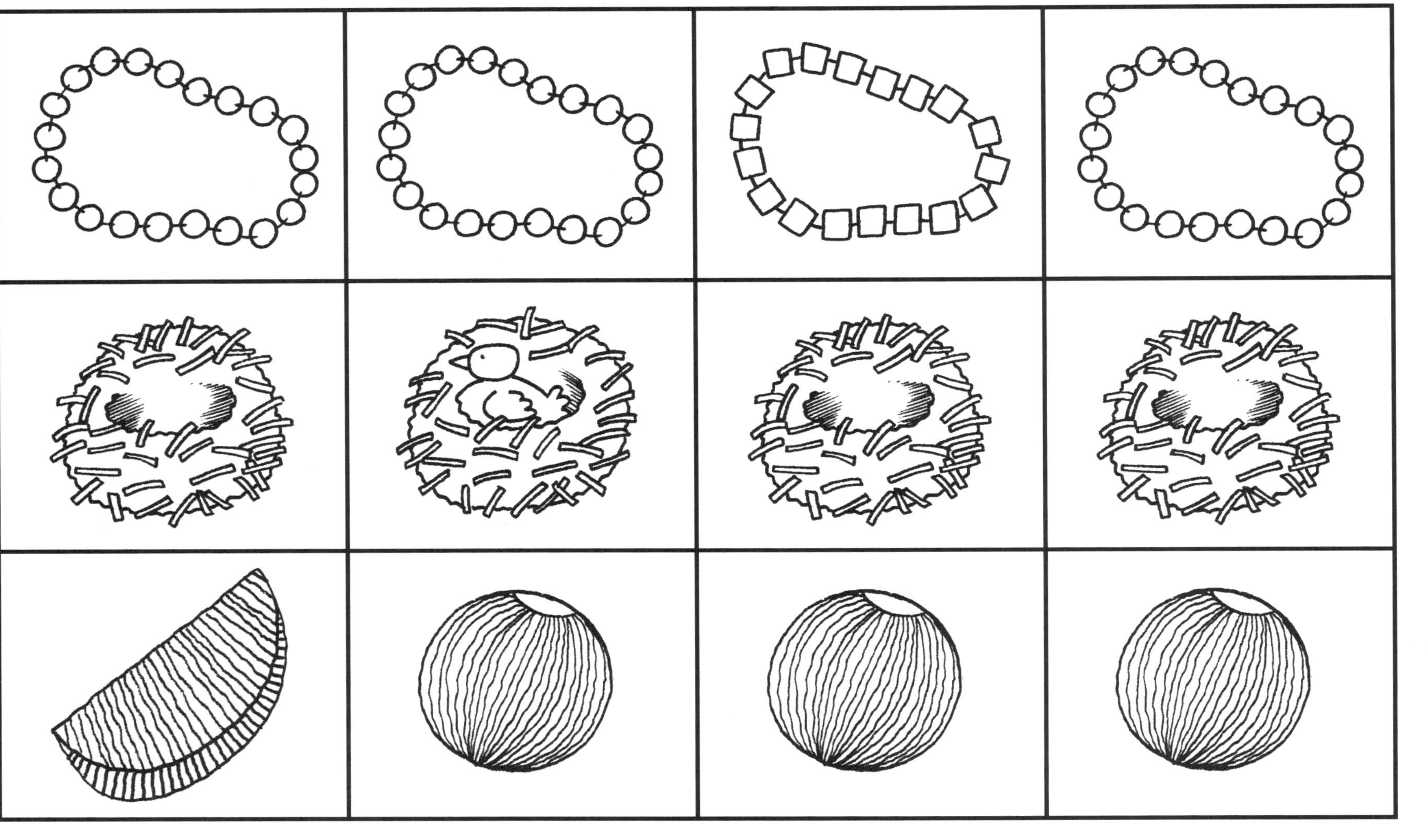

THE o SOUND

(o as in orange)

PRONUNCIATION GUIDE

To make the **o** sound, open your mouth to a round shape, dropping the chin. Say *a*, but move your lips into a circle to say *o*.

LISTENING

WHAT'S ON THE CD

- The rhymes and games for the o sound include:
  - Oranges and Lemons
  - Listening game

RHYMES AND SONGS

- Share rhymes and songs containing the **o** sound.

Saturday, Sunday

On Saturday night,
Shall be all my care
To powder my locks
And curl my hair.

On Sunday morning,
My love will come in.
When he will marry me
With a gold ring.

What are Little Boys Made of?

What are little boys made of?
What are little boys made of?
Snips and snails and puppy dog tails,
That's what little boys are made of.

What are little girls made of?
What are little girls made of?
Sugar and spice and everything nice,
That's what little girls are made of.

I Saw Three Ships

I saw three ships come sailing in
On Christmas day, on Christmas day;
I saw three ships come sailing in
On Christmas day in the morning.

And what was in those ships all three,
On Christmas day, on Christmas day?
And what was in those ships all three,
On Christmas day in the morning?

Here is the Ostrich

Here is the ostrich, straight and tall,
(Bend arm and shape fingers like a bird, with thumb as a head.)
Nodding his head above us all.
(Make thumb move in a nod.)

Here is the snake on the ground,
(Wriggle your arm around like a snake.)
Wriggling on the stones all around.

Here are the birds that fly so high,
(Move hands around, like birds flying.)
Spreading their wings across the sky.

Here is the hedgehog prickly and small,
(Clench fingers tightly in a ball.)
Rolling himself into a ball.

Here is the spider scuttling around,
(Spread fingers and move around.)
Treading so lightly on the ground.

Here are the children fast asleep,
(Rest head against hands.)
And in the night the owls do peep,
(Put fingers around the eyes in rings.)

Too-wit too-whoo, too-wit too-whoo
Too-wit too-whoo, too-wit too-whoo

On the First of March

On the first of March,
The crows begin to search,
By the first of April,
They are sitting still;
By the first of May,
They've all flown away;
Coming greedy back again,
With October's wind and rain.

Oranges and Lemons

'Oranges and lemons,' say the Bells of St Clement's.

'You owe me five farthings,' say the Bells of St Martin's.

'When will you pay me?' say the Bells of Old Bailey.

'When I grow rich,' say the Bells of Shoreditch.

'When will that be?' say the Bells of Stepney.

'I do not know,' say the Great Bells of Bow.

Here comes a candle to light you to bed,

Here comes a chopper to chop off your head

Chip chop chip chop – the last man's dead.

ACTIVITIES

Listen to the CD and ask the children if they can answer the questions. The answers are below.

- What am I? I am a very tall bird. I cannot fly. I have a very long neck. **(ostrich)**
- What am I? I live in the sea and have lots of legs. **(octopus)**

- Play an action game: an adult whispers an action to the child, remembering to emphasise the **o** sound. The child then has to act it out. Other children then try to guess the action. This is difficult, so give help and clues, so that the child is successful. For example, actions could include:
  - Jump **on** a step.
  - Jump **off** a step.
  - Peel an **orange**.
  - Make your hand and arm look like an **ostrich**.
- Look for story books which begin with the **o** sound and read them aloud to your class. For example:

Oscar Got the Blame by Tony Ross (Andersen Press Ltd)
On your Potty by Virginia Miller (Walker Books Ltd)
The Wonderful Wizard of Oz by L Frank Baum (Penguin)

- Look for non-fiction books in the library. You can find books about otters, an orchestra, octopus and ostriches.
- Find children's names beginning with the **o** sound, such as Oscar, Oliver, Oswald, Oz, Omri, Olive.
- Make an **oblong** shape on a sheet of paper. Cut out other oblongs in different sizes. Ask the children to glue them to make a shape, such as a house, windows, door and chimney.
- Ask the children to look for objects beginning with the **o** sound in their cupboards and in the supermarket. Make an **orange** jelly, drink orange juice, eat orange marmalade, try orange biscuits. (Ensure you are aware of any food allergies before commencing this activity.)

EVALUATION

- These questions are intended to assess the children's ability to hear the **o** sound. Ask them to rub the outside part of their ears before they start to listen.
- Read the following questions to the children:
  1. What sound is at the beginning of these words?
     orange, on, off, otter, octopus, office
  2. In these groups of three words, which word begins with the **o** sound?
     a) on, up, by
     b) three, four, orange
     c) can, otter, road
     d) arm, eat, ostrich
     e) picture, man, octopus
     f) off, boy, over
  3. Clap when you hear a word with the **o** sound at the beginning:
     book, orange, off, octopus, light, office, otter

EXTENSION ACTIVITY

■ As a further challenge for children you can try 'Robot talk'. A list of suggested words is given below.

- The adult says the word such as 'odd' and then says it in 'Robot talk' /o/dd/, sounding out the individual sounds. Then repeat this.
- The child then says the word, for example 'odd'. It may take a few tries to perfect the word.
- The adult then says the sounds and claps each one, for example /o/dd/. Then the child joins in.

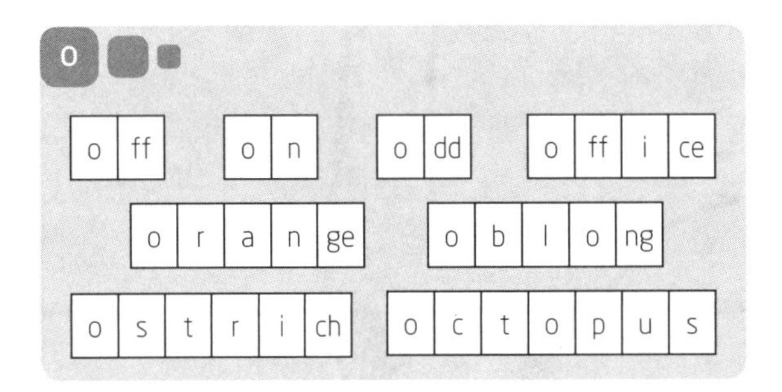

SEEING

■ Show the children photocopiable page 117 and ask them if they can identify the objects beginning with the **o** sound.

■ Make two copies of photocopiable page 117. Cut around the shapes and use them for games such as 'Snap' and 'Pairs'.

■ Ask the children to colour in or circle the objects beginning with the **o** sound on photocopiable page 118.

■ Provide the children with copies of photocopiable page 119. Ask them to complete the dot-to-dot puzzle to make a picture of an octopus.

THINKING

■ Together, make the shape of big **oranges** in the air. Make it with one arm, and then with the other arm. Try both arms together.

■ Ask the children to clap one knee with the **opposite** hand. Now clap the other knee with the other hand. Keep trying this, until you can do it easily. Then try doing 'high fives' with a friend, using one hand at a time. Clap opposite hands to music.

■ Encourage the children to experiment with the following **opposites**:

- Jump high, then jump low.
- Climb into a big box, then out of it.
- Walk forwards, walk backwards.
- Climb on a chair, climb off a chair.
- Run in big circles, run in small circles.
- Look asleep, look awake.
- Walk fast, walk slowly.
- Look happy, look sad.

■ Invite the children to imagine they are an **octopus** with eight long arms (called tentacles). Tell them to move their arms around, up and down and round about; swim around in the sea, looking for food.

■ Ask the children to imagine they are Dorothy in the story of the Wizard of **Oz**. Draw a brick road with yellow chalk on the ground. Dance up and down the road, singing.

THINKING AND REASONING SKILLS

■ Show the children the picture on photocopiable page 116 and ask them the following questions:

1. What sort of bird is this?
2. What is the bird doing?
3. Why does the bird sit on the eggs?
4. What happens when the shell breaks?
5. What is this called?
6. What is the baby bird called?
7. How will the chick feed?
8. Would you like to be an ostrich? Why/why not?
9. What other type of bird would you like to be? What colour and size would you be? Where would you live?
10. Can you make a collage of you as a bird? Use feathers, cloth and sticky paper to stick on the picture.

Words beginning with *o*

Can you guess the word beginning with ***o***?

Answers: ostrich, orange, octopus, oblong, otter, ox

Spot the *o* sound

Put a ring around or colour in the pictures beginning with ***o***.

Dot-to-dot octopus

Join the dots to make the shape of an octopus.
How many arms does an octopus have?

THE p SOUND

(p as in pig)

PRONUNCIATION GUIDE

To make the **p** sound, the lips are pressed together, then opened to allow the breath to 'pop' out.

LISTENING

WHAT'S ON THE CD

- The rhymes and games for the p sound include:
  - Polly Put the Kettle on
  - Half a Pound of Tuppenny Rice
  - Listening game

RHYMES AND SONGS

- Share rhymes and songs containing the **p** sound.

Pussy Cat, Pussy Cat

Pussy cat, pussy cat, where have you been?
I've been to London to look at the queen.
Pussy cat, pussy cat, what did you there?
I frightened a little mouse under her chair.

Polly Put the Kettle on

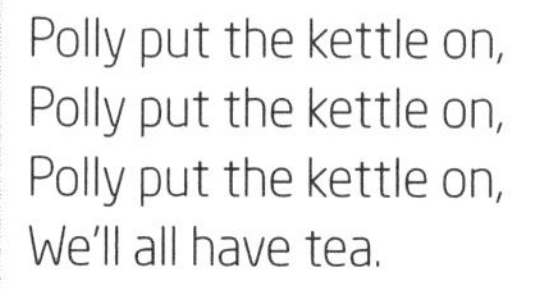

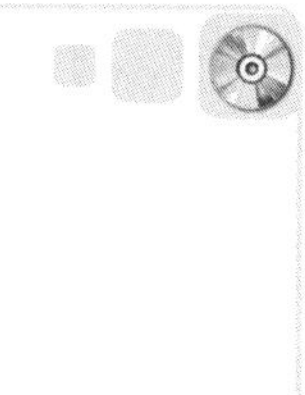

Polly put the kettle on,
Polly put the kettle on,
Polly put the kettle on,
We'll all have tea.

Sukey take it off again,
Sukey take it off again,
Sukey take it off again,
They've all gone away.

Pat-a-Cake, Pat-a-Cake

Pat-a-cake, Pat-a-cake, baker's man
Bake me a cake as fast as you can;
Pat it and prick it and mark it with 'B',
Put it in the oven for baby and me.

Tongue twister

Peter Piper picked a peck of pickled pepper;
Did Peter Piper pick a peck of pickled peper?
If Peter Piper picked a peck of pickled pepper,
Where's the peck of pickled pepper Peter Piper picked?

Half a Pound of Tuppenny Rice

Half a pound of tuppenny rice,
Half a pound of treacle.
That's the way the money goes,
Pop! goes the weasel.

Up and down the City road,
In and out the Eagle,
That's the way the money goes,
Pop! goes the weasel.

Every night when I go out
The monkey's on the table
Take a stick and knock it off
Pop! goes the weasel.

A penny for a ball of thread
Another for a needle,
That's the way the money goes,
Pop! goes the weasel.

All around the cobbler's bench
the monkey chased the people;
The donkey thought 'twas all in fun,
Pop! goes the weasel.

Pease Pudding Hot

Pease pudding hot, pease pudding cold,
Pease pudding in the pot – nine days old.

Some like it hot, some like it cold,
Some like it in the pot – nine days old.

Peter Works with One Hammer

Peter works with one hammer, one hammer,
one hammer,
Peter works with one hammer, all day long.

Peter works with two hammers...

Peter works with three hammers...

Peter works with four hammers...

Peter's very tired now...

Peter's going to sleep now...
...all night long.

Peter's waking up now, up now, up now
Peter's waking up now, this fine day.

Action rhyme
The children hammer with one finger (one hammer), then two fingers, and so on.
In the final verses the children should yawn, then go to sleep and jump up again.

Peter, Peter, Pumpkin-Eater

Peter, Peter, pumpkin-eater,
Had a wife and couldn't keep her;
He put her in a pumpkin shell,
And there he kept her very well.

ACTIVITIES

Listen to the CD and ask the children if they can guess the following sounds:
- A **pig**
- A **parrot**
- A **piano**

■ Play an action game: an adult whispers an action to the child, remembering to emphasise the **p** sound. The child then has to act it out. Other children then try to guess the action. This is difficult, so give help and clues, so that the child is successful. For example, actions could include:
- **Paint** a **picture**.
- **Peel** an orange.
- **Plant** seeds.
- **Pour** a drink.
- **Play** with a **parachute**.
- Waddle like a **penguin**.
- **Play** with a **puppet**.
- **Play** the **piano**.
- **Play pass** the **parcel**.
- **Push** a **pram**.

■ Look for story books which begin with the **p** sound and read them aloud to your class. For example:

The Three Little Pigs (Ladybird and others)
Each Peach, Pear, Plum by Allan and Janet Ahlberg (Viking Children's Books)
Peepo by Allan and Janet Ahlberg (Puffin Books)
Pinocchio (Ladybird and others)
The Runaway Pancake (Ladybird and others)
That's not my Puppy by Fiona Watt and Rachel Wells (Usborne Publishing Ltd)
Pumpkin Soup by Helen Cooper (Corgi)
The Magic Porridge Pot (Ladybird Tales and others)
Puss in Boots (Ladybird Tales)
The Princess and the Pea (Ladybird Tales)
Peter and the Wolf (Ladybird and others)

■ Look for non-fiction books in the library. You can find books about penguins, pandas and peacocks.
■ Find children's names beginning with the **p** sound, such as Peter, Paul, Patrick, Paige, Penina, Pazit.
■ Use pictures from magazines and catalogues of things beginning with the **p** sound.
■ Encourage the children to make a **post** office in the role-play corner. Ask them what they will need for their post office: for example, a post box with collection times, **paper**, stamps, a weighing machine, envelopes to post, some boxes for **parcels**, **postcards**, **pens**, **pencils**, a telephone, **play** money.
■ Make some **play dough**, using the following recipe:

Ingredients
1 cup water
1 cup plain flour
2 tablespoons cream of tartar
½ cup of salt
1 tablespoon cooking oil
Food colouring

What to do
1. Mix all the ingredients (except the colouring) in a pan.
2. An adult should then heat the mixture over a medium heat, stirring all the time until it comes together as a dough.
3. Allow to cool a little and knead the dough until it is smooth and pliable.
4. Divide the dough into two or more pieces. Use food colouring to colour each piece.
5. Wrap the dough in cling film, then store it in an airtight container or plastic bag in the fridge.

EVALUATION

■ These questions are intended to assess the children's ability to hear the **p** sound. Ask them to rub the outside part of their ears before they start to listen.
■ Read the following questions to the children:

1. What sound is at the beginning of these words?
   pig, parcel, paint, pear, penguin, peacock, pencil, pen
2. In these groups of three words, which word begins with the **p** sound?
   a) pig, rat, hen
   b) fan, smell, puppy
   c) tooth, party, stamp
   d) peach, reach, beach
   e) cat, bag, pat
   f) tail, pail, whale
3. Clap when you hear a word with a **p** sound at the beginning:
   pin, pen, pencil, paper, dog, peach, pink, pancake, hen

EXTENSION ACTIVITY

■ As a further challenge for children you can try 'Robot talk'. A list of suggested words is given below.

■ The adult says the word such as 'pig' and then says it in 'Robot talk' /p/i/g/, sounding out the individual sounds. Then repeat this.

■ The child then says the word, for example 'pig'. It may take a few tries to perfect the word.

■ The adult then says the sounds and claps each one, for example /p/i/g/. Then the child joins in.

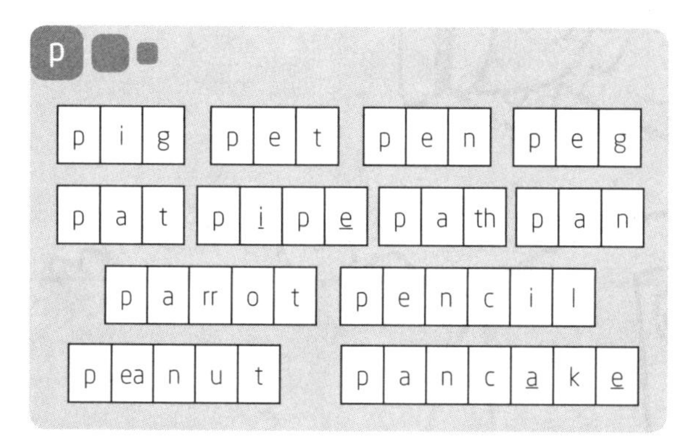

SEEING

■ Show the children photocopiable page 125 and ask them if they can identify the objects beginning with the **p** sound.

■ Make two copies of photocopiable page 125. Cut around the shapes and use them for games such as 'Snap' and 'Pairs'.

■ Can the children find five differences in the second picture on photocopiable page 126?

■ Show the children photocopiable page 127. Ask them to match the pairs of objects either by tracing with a finger, or drawing a pencil line.

THINKING

■ Find a big piece of old wallpaper. Lay it on the ground with the white side up. With **pink paint** and a large brush, ask the children to paint all over the **paper** and let it dry. Encourage them to use one hand, then the other to hold the **paintbrush**. Make **pictures** of animals and birds, beginning with the **p** sound, and stick them on the pink background.

■ Ask the children to sit on a stool or chair, and **pretend** to **pedal** a bike – holding onto the handlebars and making their legs go really fast.

■ Invite the children to jump up and down like **popcorn popping** in a **pan**.

■ Encourage the children to imagine they are a **prince** or **princess**, going to a ball in the **palace**. Tell them they have to decide what to wear from their wardrobe – a nice suit or dress. Ask them: *What colour is your outfit? What about your shoes? Do you need anything else for the ball?* (For example, princesses might want a tiara, bag, gloves; princes might want a hat or handkerchief.) Encourage them to dance around as if they are at the ball.

■ Imagine the class is having a **party**. Ask: *What food will you give to your friends? What games will you* ***play****? Imagine playing* ***pass*** *the* ***parcel****. Did you win the* ***prize****? Can you set up a tea party in the home corner?*

THINKING AND REASONING SKILLS

■ Show the children the picture on photocopiable page 124 and ask them the following questions:

1. What type of van is this?
2. What is this man's job?
3. What colour is a post box?
4. What is the man collecting?
5. Why do people write letters?
6. What do you need if you want to write and post a letter?
7. Have you ever had a letter sent to you? Why?
8. Was there anything in the envelope? How did you feel when you opened the letter?
9. How do you thank someone who has sent you a gift?
10. What happens to a letter after you have dropped it in the post box?
11. 'Write' a letter to your friend, inviting them to a party. How will they feel when they get your invitation?

Post

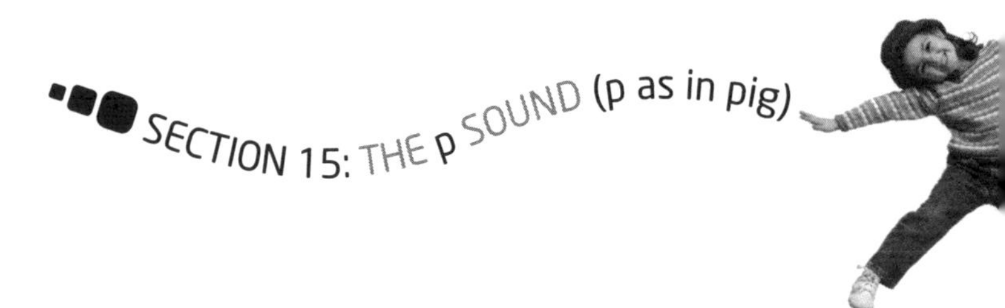

Words beginning with *p*

Can you guess the word beginning with ***p***?

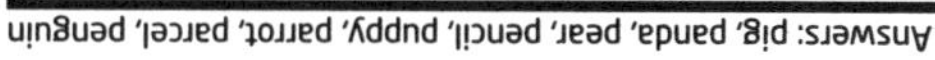

Spot the difference

Can you find five things that are different in the second picture?

Matching game

Join the pictures that are the same.

THE qu SOUND

(qu as in queen)

PRONUNCIATION GUIDE

To make the **qu** (/k/w/) sound, put your lips forward and make the sound at the back of your mouth.

LISTENING

WHAT'S ON THE CD

- The rhymes and games for the qu sound include:
  - Five Little Ducks
  - Listening game

RHYMES AND SONGS

- Share rhymes and songs containing the qu sound.

The Queen of Hearts

The Queen of Hearts
She made some tarts,
All on a summer's day;
The Knave of Hearts
He stole the tarts,
And took them clean away!
The King of Hearts
Called for the tarts,
And beat the Knave full sore.;
The Knave of Hearts
Brought back the tarts,
And vowed he'd steal no more.

Five Little Ducks Went out to Play

Five little ducks went out to play,
Wibble wobble, wibble wobble to and fro,
But the one little duck,
With the feather on his back,
He led the others with a quack, quack, quack,
Quack, quack, quack
Quack, quack, quack.
He led the others with a quack, quack, quack.

Mary, Mary, Quite Contrary

Mary, Mary, quite contrary,
How does your garden grow?
Silver bells and cockle-shells,
And pretty maids all of a row.

Hector Protector

Hector Protector was dressed all in green;
Hector Protector was sent to the Queen.
The Queen did not like him,
No more did the King;
So Hector Protector was sent back again.

Five Little Ducks

Five little ducks
Went out one day,
Over the hill and far away.
Mother duck said,
'Quack, quack, quack, quack.'
But only four little ducks came back.

Four little ducks
Went out one day,
Over the hill and far away.
Mother duck said,
'Quack, quack, quack, quack.'
But only three little ducks came back.

Three little ducks
Went out one day,
Over the hill and far away.
Mother duck said,
'Quack, quack, quack, quack.'
But only two little ducks came back.

Two little ducks
Went out one day,
Over the hill and far away.
Mother duck said,
'Quack, quack, quack, quack.'
But only one little duck came back.

One little duck
Went out one day,
Over the hill and far away.
Mother duck said,
'Quack, quack, quack, quack.'
But none of the five little ducks came back.

Sad mother duck
Went out one day,
Over the hill and far away.
The sad mother duck said
'Quack, quack, quack, quack.'
And all of the five little ducks came back.

Pussy Cat, Pussy Cat

Pussy cat, pussy cat, where have you been?
I've been to London to look at the queen.
Pussy cat, pussy cat, what did you there?
I frightened a little mouse under her chair.

Miss Polly Had a Dolly

Miss Polly had a dolly,
Who was sick, sick, sick.
So she phoned for the doctor
To be quick, quick, quick.

The doctor came
With his bag and his hat,
And he rapped the door
With a rat-a-tat tat.

He looked at the dolly
And he shook his head.
Then he said 'Miss Polly,
Put her straight to bed.'

He wrote on a paper
For a pill, pill, pill.
'I'll be back in the morning
With my bill, bill, bill.'

Miss Polly actions

Verse 1: Children rock the dolly in their arms.
Verse 2: Children knock on an imaginary door.
Verse 3: Children shake their heads and wag their fingers.
Verse 4: Children pretend to write on a piece of paper.

ACTIVITIES

Listen to the CD and ask the children if they can guess the following sound:
- Ducks **quacking**.

■ Play an action game: an adult whispers an action to the child, remembering to emphasise the **qu** sound. The child then has to act it out. Other children then try to guess the action. This is difficult, so give help and clues, so that the child is successful. For example, actions could include:
- Run **quickly**.
- Step on **quicksand**.
- Be very **quiet**.
- Wrap yourself in a **quilt**.
- **Quiver** like a jelly.
- Cut a cake into **quarters**.

■ Look for story books which begin with the **qu** sound and read them aloud to your class. For example:

The Snow Queen by Hans Christian Andersen, (Red Fox)
Queen of the Scene by Queen Latifah (HarperCollins Children's Books)
The Queen's Knickers by Nicholas Allan (Red Fox)
The Quangle Wangle's Hat by Edward Lear (Walker Books Ltd)

■ Look for non-fiction books in the library. You can find books about Queen Elizabeth and her family, kings and queens in history, quicksand, and making quilts.

■ Find children's names beginning with the **qu** sound, such as Quentin, Quincy, Quinn, Quennell, Queenie , Quasar, Qwara.

■ Ask the children to draw a picture of a **queen**, wearing her crown and sitting on her throne.

■ Divide a cake, an apple or a pancake into halves, then **quarters**. Share the quarters among four friends or four dolls. (Ensure you are aware of any food allergies before commencing this activity.)

■ Remind the children of the rhyme about the **Queen** of Hearts baking some tarts. Together, find a recipe for jam tarts and make them.

EVALUATION

■ These questions are intended to assess children's ability to hear the **qu** sound. Ask them to rub the outside part of their ears before they start to listen.

■ Read the following questions to the children:

1. What sound is at the beginning of these words?
   queen, quack, quilt, quarrel, quiet, quite, quarter, quill, quicksand
2. In these groups of three words, which word begins with the **qu** sound?
   a) queen, throne, crown
   b) bed, quilt, girl
   c) run, quick, house
   d) boy, apple, quack
   e) write, pencil, quill
   f) cake, quarter, knife
3. Clap when you hear a word with the **qu** sound at the beginning:
   queen, quack, quilt, book, quiet, quarter, boy, quill, quicksand

EXTENSION ACTIVITY

■ As a further challenge for children you can try 'Robot talk'. A list of suggested words is given below. (Please note **qu** is two sounds, /k/w/.)

- The adult says the word such as 'quill' and then says it in 'Robot talk' /q/u/i/ll/, sounding out the individual sounds. Then repeat this.
- The child then says the word, for example 'quill'. It may take a few tries to perfect the word.
- The adult then says the sounds and claps each one, for example /q/u/i/ll/. Then the child joins in.

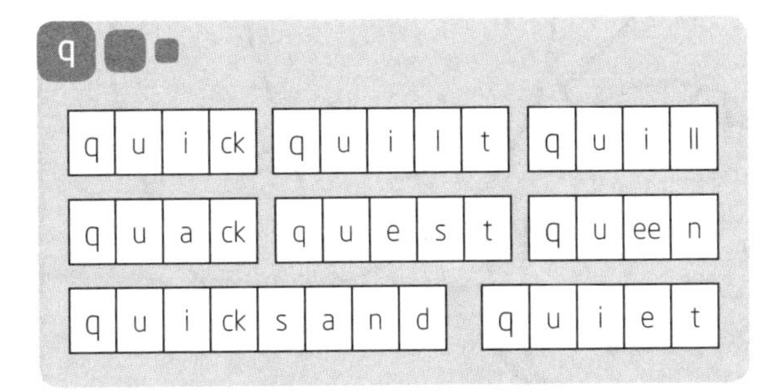

SEEING

■ Show the children photocopiable page 133 and ask them if they can identify the objects beginning with the **qu** sound.

■ Make two copies of photocopiable page 133. Cut around the shapes and use them for games such as 'Snap' and 'Pairs'.

■ Can the children find the five differences in the second picture on photocopiable page 134?

■ Display photocopiable page 135. Ask the children to help the explorer find his way through the quicksand by following the path with a finger, or using a pencil. Encourage them to move their eyes from left to right as they complete the activity.

THINKING

■ Ask the children to draw a large **queen's** crown (with a jagged edge at the top) in the air with one of their hands. Then ask them to draw the same crown with their other hand.

■ Draw a large square on the ground with chalk. Use the chalk to divide the square into **quarters**. Then draw a circle and oblong and divide them into quarters. Ask the children if they can hop around the quarters of a shape, without putting their foot down on the ground. Try it with either foot.

■ Encourage the children to be a **quivering** jelly, making every bit of them shake, shiver and quiver.

■ Put a mat on the floor for each child. Tell them to imagine they are an explorer in the desert. They know there is **quicksand** in the space between them and the mat. Encourage them to test the ground with their feet, to make sure it is safe. When they reach the mat safely they should show how happy they are.

■ Ask the children to imagine they are the **queen**, walking around with a heavy crown on their head. If appropriate, they could put a book on their head to feel how difficult it is to walk without dropping the crown. How **quickly** can they walk without dropping the book? Tell them to put their arms out to help them to balance.

■ Encourage the children to imagine they are the **queen** in the rhyme 'Pussy cat, pussy cat, where have you been?' What would they do if they found a little mouse under their chair?

THINKING AND REASONING SKILLS

■ Show the children the picture on photocopiable page 132 and ask them the following questions:

1. Who is in the picture?
2. What is the mummy doing?
3. What has she in her hand?
4. What is she going to share out?
5. How many children are there?
6. How many pieces of cake are there?
7. What is every share called?
8. Will the mummy get a share of the cake?
9. Why might she not want a share?
10. Will there be any cake left over?
11. Do you like sharing with your friends?
12. How do they thank you?
13. Do you like being kind to other people?
14. How do you feel when someone is kind to you?

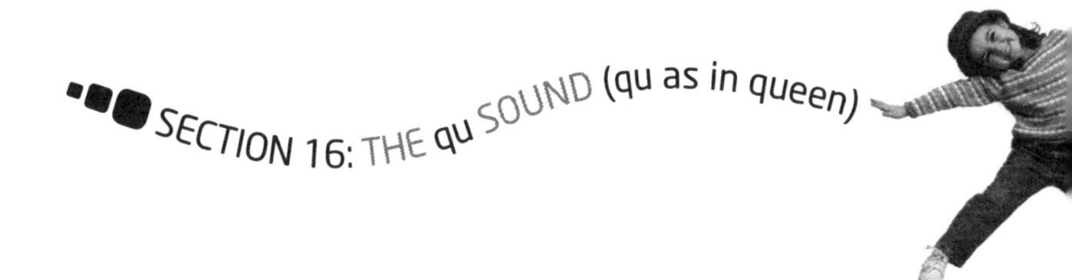

Words beginning with *qu*

Can you guess the word beginning with ***qu***?

Answers: queen, quilt, quarrel, choir, queue, quarter, quicksand, quack

Spot the difference

Can you find five things that are different in the second picture?

Help the explorer

Help the explorer to miss the quicksand, and get safely to his tent.

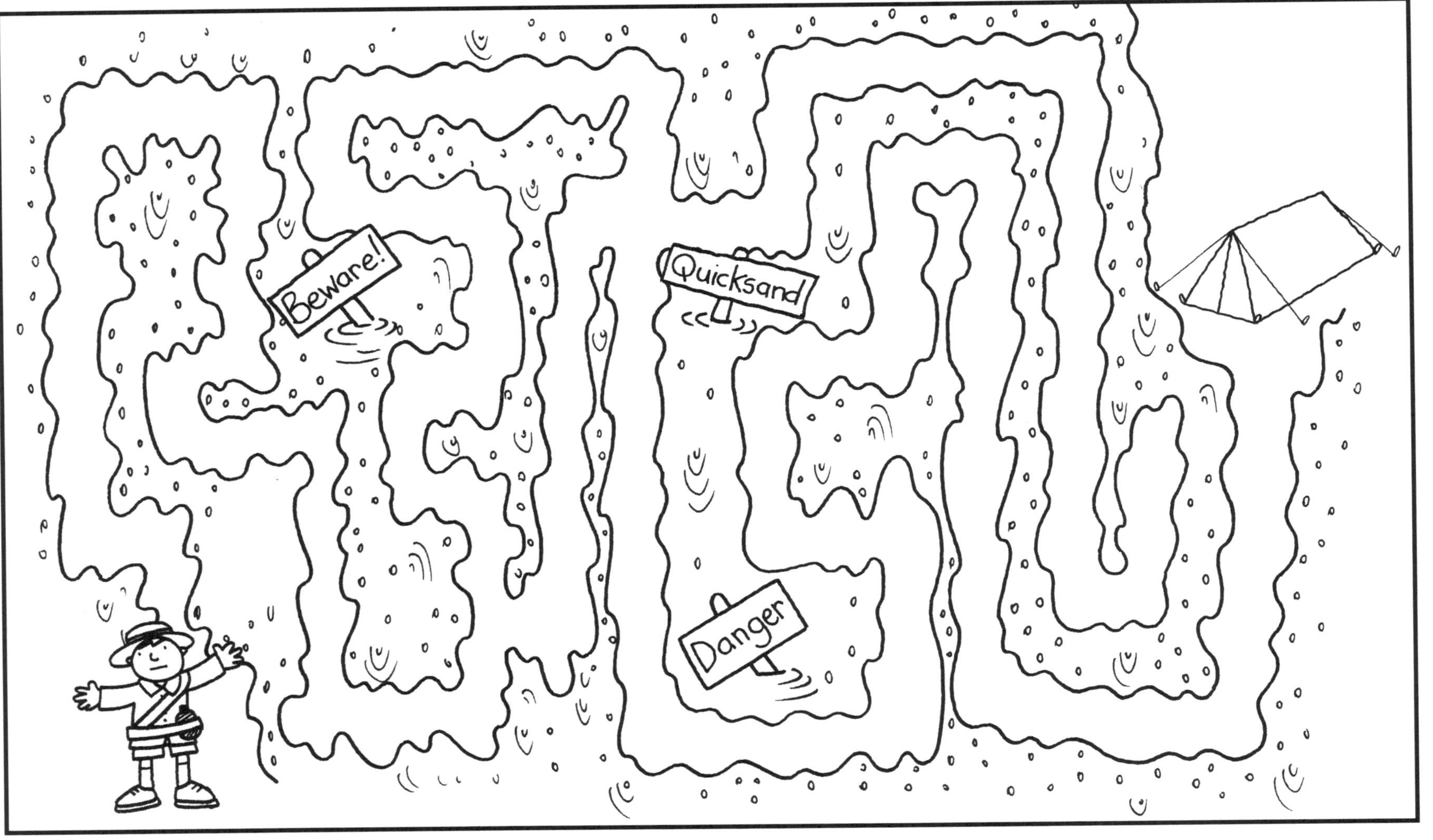

THE r SOUND

(r as in rabbit)

PRONUNCIATION GUIDE

To make the **r** sound, the tongue lifts up at the back of your mouth and becomes slightly 's'-shaped. The tongue should not touch the top of the mouth. The sound is made in the throat.

LISTENING

WHAT'S ON THE CD

- The rhymes and games for the r sound include:
  - Round and Round the Garden
  - Row, Row, Row Your Boat
  - Listening game

RHYMES AND SONGS

- Share rhymes and songs containing the **r** sound.

Rain, Rain, Go Away

Rain, rain, go away,
Come again another day.
Little Johnny wants to play;
Rain, rain, go to Spain,
Never show your face again!

Red Sky at Night

Red sky at night,
Shepherd's delight;
Red sky at morning,
Shepherd's warning.

Round is an Apple

Round is an apple,
Round is a plum,
Round is a doughnut, and the top of a drum.
Round is a lollipop,
Round is a ring,
Round is a circle and the crown of a king.

Rock-a-bye Baby

Rock-a-bye baby on the treetop,
When the wind blows the cradle will rock,
When the bough breaks the cradle will fall,
And down will come baby, cradle and all.

Round and Round the Garden

Round and round the garden,
(Trace circles with your fingers on the child's hand.)
Like a teddy bear.
One step, two steps,
And tickle you under there.
(Tickle under the arm.)

Round and Round the Rugged Rock

Round and round the rugged rock
The ragged rascal ran.

Ring Around the Rosy

Ring around the rosy
A pocketful of posies
'Ashes, Ashes'
We all fall down!

Or

Ring-a-ring o' Roses

Ring-a-ring o' roses
A pocket full of posies
'A-tishoo! A-tishoo!'
We all fall down!

Row, Row, Row Your Boat

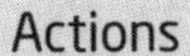

Row, row, row your boat
Gently down the stream.
Merrily, merrily, merrily, merrily
Life is but a dream.

Actions
The children sit opposite each other in pairs on the floor, with their legs stretched out in front of them. They should sit toe to toe. They then hold hands and gently pull each other backwards and forwards, as if rowing a boat.

ACTIVITIES

■ Make a **recording** of the children saying, 'Round and round the rugged rock'. Ask the children if they can recognise their voices.

Listen to the CD and ask the children if they can guess what the sound effects are. The questions and answers are below.
- What is the telephone doing? (**ringing**)
- What is the lion doing? (**roaring**)
- What is the weather like? (**raining**)

■ Play an action game: an adult whispers an action to the child, remembering to emphasise the **r** sound. The child then has to act it out. Other children then try to guess the action. This is difficult, so give help and clues, so that the child is successful. For example, actions could include:
- **Read** a book.
- **Run** around.
- **Race** your friend.
- **Roll** on the floor.
- **Ring** a bell.
- **Row** a boat.
- Jump like a **rabbit**.
- **Rake** up the leaves.
- **Reel** in a fish with your fishing line.
- Pull the **reins** on your horse.
- **Rub** your hands together.

■ Look for story books which begin with the **r** sound and read them aloud to your class. For example:

Revolting Rhymes by Roald Dahl (Puffin Books)
The Rascally Cake by Jeanne Willis and Korky Paul (Puffin Books)
Rover by Michael Rosen and Neal Layton (Bloomsbury Publishing)
The Tale of Peter Rabbit by Beatrix Potter (Frederick Warne Publishers Ltd)
Rosie's Walk by Pat Hutchins (Scholastic Children's Books)
Rapunzel (Ladybird Tales)
Little Red Riding Hood (Ladybird and others)
Little Rabbit Runaway by Harry Horse (Puffin Books)

■ Look for non-fiction books in the library. You can find books about rabbits, rockets, rivers, rain and rainbows.

■ Find children's names beginning with the **r** sound, such as Ryan, Rasheeq, Reuben, Rachel, Ruth, Rina.

■ Use pictures from magazines and catalogues of things beginning with the **r** sound.

■ Find out about **Ramadan**. Ramadan is the ninth month of the Muslim calendar. During this month, Muslims do not eat or drink during daylight hours. This is called fasting. Each day during Ramadan, Muslim families get up early before sunrise to eat a morning meal together and to perform a special prayer. Once the sun has set, families gather together again to eat their evening meal.

■ Buy some **ready-made**, sweet shortcrust pastry. Show the children how to use a **rolling** pin to roll it out. Use different shapes of cutters to make little biscuits. Make icing from icing sugar, water and colouring. Decorate with little pieces of fruit. Or you could make your own recipe, by changing the topping (for example, you could try **raspberry** jam instead of icing). (Ensure you are aware of any food allergies before commencing this activity.)

■ Start a **recycling** bank, if you do not already have one. Ask the children to collect drink cans, paper, newspaper, envelopes, cardboard and plastic bottles. Use the special bins from your local council or take the items to a local recycling facility.

■ Make a **rainbow** using a glass prism and a sprinkler or garden hose on a sunny day. Talk about the colours in the rainbow.

EVALUATION

■ These questions are intended to assess children's ability to hear the **r** sound. Ask them to rub the outside part of their ears before they start to listen.

■ Read the following questions to the children:

1. What sound is at the beginning of these words?
   rabbit, ring, rocket, robot, ribbon, rat, roof, rainbow, rock, radio
2. In these groups of three words, which word begins with the **r** sound?
   a) rabbit, sock, boat
   b) robot, door, floor
   c) donkey, rock, cat
   d) pen, roof, tooth
   e) bun, dig, ribbon
   f) light, white, right
3. Clap when you hear a word with the **r** sound at the beginning:
   rabbit, ring, rocking horse , robot, coat, ribbon, rat, roof, hat, rainbow

EXTENSION ACTIVITY

■ As a further challenge for children you can try 'Robot talk'. A list of suggested words is given below.

■ The adult says the word such as 'red' and then says it in 'Robot talk' /r/e/d/, sounding out the individual sounds. Then repeat this.

■ The child then says the word, for example 'red'. It may take a few tries to perfect the word.

■ The adult then says the sounds and claps each one, for example /r/e/d/. Then the child joins in.

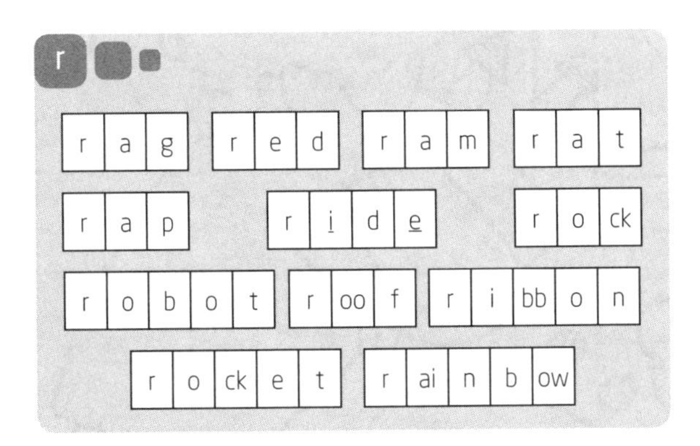

SEEING

■ Show the children photocopiable page 141 and ask them if they can identify the objects beginning with the **r** sound.

■ Make two copies of photocopiable page 141. Cut around the shapes and use them for games such as 'Snap' and 'Pairs'.

■ Ask the children to match the shadows with the correct shapes on photocopiable page 142.

■ Display photocopiable page 143. Ask the children to help the rabbit find its burrow, either by tracing the path with their fingers, or with a pencil. Encourage them to move their eyes from left to right as they complete the activity.

THINKING

■ Find a mat or carpet. Can the children **roll** on this? Can they roll over? Ask them to try rolling quickly and then slowly.

■ Encourage the children to **ride** toy vehicles such as tricycles.

■ Invite the children to **run** a **race** with their friends. How fast can they run? Time the children by counting out loud. Continue to time them to find out if they are becoming faster. You can keep a record of how fast the children run.

■ Encourage the children to do bunny jumps around the **room** or playground. Ask: *Why are they called bunny jumps?*

■ Ask the children to imagine they are a **rabbit**, jumping around the field, looking for lettuce to eat, sniffing and twitching their whiskers, sitting up with their front paws in the air, and playing chasing games with the other rabbits.

THINKING AND REASONING SKILLS

Show the children the pictures on photocopiable page 140 and ask them the following questions:

PICTURE ONE

1. Who is in the picture?
2. What is happening outside?
3. Does the boy look happy?
4. Why is he unhappy?

PICTURE TWO

1. What has happened now?
2. Where has the boy gone?
3. Is he still in the house?
4. What games do you think he is playing?
5. Will he have a smiling face or a frowning face?
6. How do you feel when it is raining?
7. Do you go out and splash in the puddles?
8. What do you wear to play in the rain?
9. Draw a picture of you splashing in puddles.
10. Make a weather chart for every day. Collect the rain in a plastic bucket and pour it into a clear plastic bottle. Make a measure on the side of the bottle by marking regular intervals. Write down the number for every day on a chart. Why does the rain dry up from the ground?

140

SCHOLASTIC

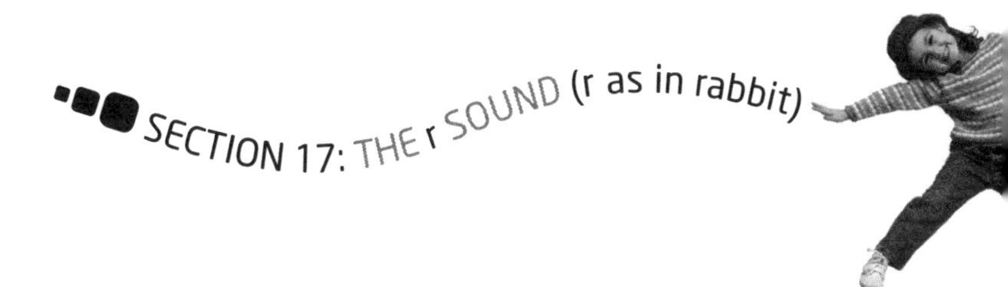

Words beginning with *r*

Can you guess the word beginning with ***r***?

Answers: rabbit, ring, rocket, robot, ribbon, rat, rock, radio

Match the shadow

Match the picture to its shadow.

Help the rabbit

Help the rabbit to find its burrow, and to escape from the fox.

THE s SOUND

(s as in sand)

PRONUNCIATION GUIDE

To make the **s** sound, open your mouth a little bit, and put your tongue flat behind your teeth, holding the teeth together. Force air out to hiss like a snake!

LISTENING

WHAT'S ON THE CD

- The rhymes and games for the s sound include:
  - Simple Simon
  - Six Salty Sausages
  - Listening game

RHYMES AND SONGS

- Share rhymes and songs containing the **s** sound.

Simple Simon

Simple Simon met a pieman,
Going to the fair,
Says Simple Simon to the pieman,
Let me taste your ware.

Says the pieman to Simple Simon,
Show me first your penny,
Says Simple Simon to the pieman
Indeed I have not any.

Sing a Song of Sixpence

Sing a song of sixpence, a pocket full of rye,
Four and twenty blackbirds baked in a pie.
When the pie was opened, the birds began to sing,
Was not that a dainty dish to set before the king?

The king was in his counting-house, counting out his money,
The queen was in the parlour, eating bread and honey,
The maid was in the garden, hanging out the clothes,
Along came a blackbird and snapped off her nose.

Tongue Twister

She sells seashells on the sea shore.

A Sailor Went to Sea, Sea, Sea

A sailor went to sea, sea, sea,
To see what he could see, see, see,
But all that he could see, see, see,
Was the bottom of the deep blue sea, sea, sea.

See-Saw Marjory Daw

See-saw Marjory Daw,
Johnny shall have a new master;
He shall have a penny a day,
Because he can't work any faster.

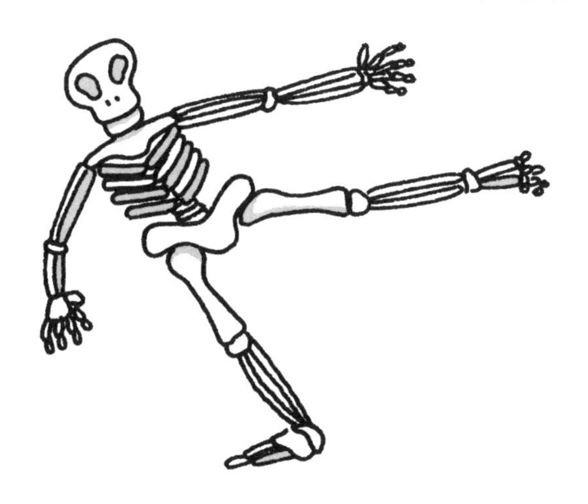

I'm a Scary Skeleton

I'm a scary skeleton
And I look just like you;
I sleep and walk, I laugh and talk
And move my body too.
My head is on my shoulders,
My neck's between the two,
I've got two eyes, a mouth, a nose,
And two ears just like you.
I'm a skeleton, I am your friend, you see.
I live inside you, so don't be scared of me!
I've got a bony body,
As everybody knows,
Two bony legs, two bony feet,
And ten small bony toes.
I've got two big bony knees,
To help me sit or stand,
Five bony little fingers,
Are on each big bony hand.
I'm a skeleton, I am your friend, you see,
I live inside you, so don't be scared of me!
I'm a skeleton, I am your friend, you see
I live inside you, so don't be scared of me.

Five Little Snowmen

Five little snowmen standing round my door.
This one melted and then there were four.
Four little snowmen beneath a green tree.
This one melted and then there were three.
Three little snowmen all have mittens blue.
This one melted and then there were two.
Two little snowmen standing in the sun.
This one melted and then there was one.
One little snowman started to run.
He melted away and then there were none.

Action game
Hold up five fingers and as each little snowman melts take away one finger, until you are left with just a fist shape.

Six Salty Sausages

Six salty sausages
Sizzling in a pan
Up jumped one and off he ran.
Put him back as fast as you can.
Six salty sausages
Sizzling in a pan

Five salty sausages...

Four salty sausages...

Three salty sausages...

Two salty sausages...

One salty sausage...

No salty sausages...

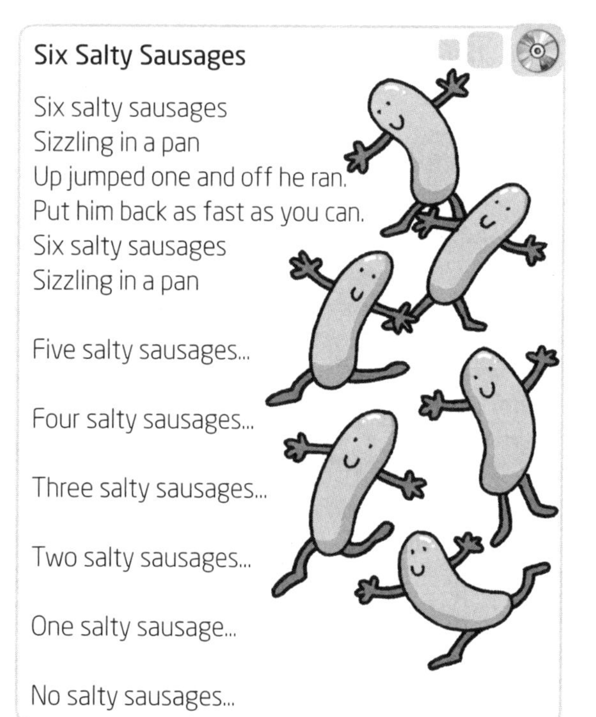

ACTIVITIES

Listen to the CD and ask the children if they can guess what the sound effects are. Questions and answers are below.

- What is the person doing? (**snoring**)
- What are the children doing in the water? (**splashing**)
- Which animal is making this sound? (**snake**)

- Play an action game: an adult whispers an action to the child, remembering to emphasise the **s** sound. The child then has to act it out. Other children then try to guess the action. This is difficult, so give help and clues, so that the child is successful. For example, actions could include:
  - **Snore**.
  - **Sleep**.
  - **Splash** in a puddle.
  - **Swim**.
  - **Stamp** your feet.
  - **Swing** your arms.
  - **Sweep** up the leaves.
  - **Sniff** around like a dog.
  - **Smile**.
  - **Sink** down.
  - **Stir** a pot.
  - **Squeeze** your hand.
  - **Stand** up.
- Look for story books which begin with the **s** sound and read them aloud to your class. For example:

The Sandcastle by MP Robertson (Frances Lincoln Children's Books)
Silly Sally by Audrey Wood (Harcourt Children's Books)
The Tiny Seed by Eric Carle (Puffin Books)
The Snowman by Raymond Briggs (Puffin Books)
Spot Can Count by Eric Hill (Puffin Books)
Where's Spot? by Eric Hill (Frederick Warne Publishers Ltd)
Stellaluna by Janell Cannon (Red Wagon Books)
The Very Busy Spider by Eric Carle (Grosset & Dunlap)

- Look for non-fiction books in the library. You can find books about stars, seeds, spiders and snakes.
- Find children's names beginning with the **s** sound, such as Sam, Scott, Steven, Simon, Siddeeqi, Saul, Seth, Sandra, Susan, Sally, Sophie, Sameera, Sara.
- Use pictures from magazines and catalogues of things beginning with the **s** sound. Do any toys begin with **s**?
- Tell the children that before you make some **sandwiches**, they must use **soap** and water to **scrub** their hands and nails. Ask the children why they should wash their hands before they prepare food. Make sandwiches with your favourite **spread**. Cut the sandwiches into **shapes** with cutters. (Ensure you are aware of any food allergies or dietary requirements before commencing this activity.)
- Cook some **spaghetti** in boiling water with a little olive oil. Use a jar of **special** tomato **sauce** for spaghetti to make it **scrumptious**. (Again, check for any food allergies or dietary requirements before you start this activity.)

EVALUATION

- These questions are intended to assess the children's ability to hear the **s** sound. Ask them to rub the outside part of their ears before they start to listen.
- Read the following questions to the children:
  1. What sound is at the beginning of these words?
     snake, scissors, sun, snail, snowman, star, spider, stool, strawberries, sandcastle
  2. In these groups of three words, which word begins with the **s** sound?
     a) sun, toy, goal
     b) fly, bird, spider
     c) rope, star, puppy
     d) stool, back, fish
     e) hat, mat, snail
     f) shake, jelly, scissors
  3. Clap when you hear a word with the **s** sound at the beginning:
     spider, stool, pool, strawberries, sandcastle, rabbit, sun

EXTENSION ACTIVITY

- As a further challenge for children you can try 'Robot talk'. A list of suggested words is given below.
  - The adult says the word such as 'sun' and then says it in 'Robot talk' /s/u/n/, sounding out the individual sounds. Then repeat this.
  - The child then says the word, for example 'sun'.

It may take a few tries to perfect the word.

■ The adult then says the sounds and claps each one, for example /s/u/n/. Then the child joins in.

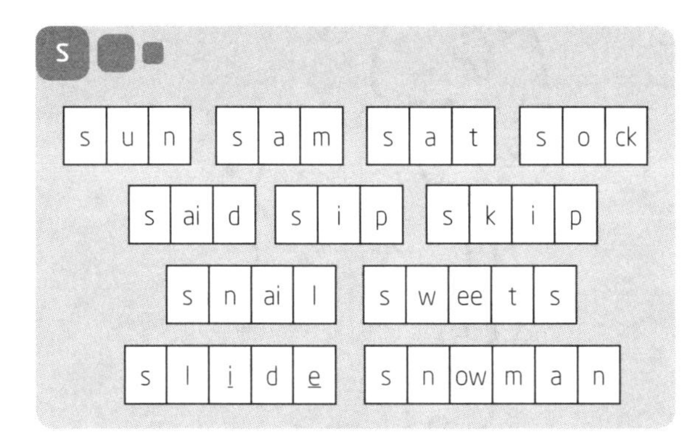

SEEING

■ Show the children photocopiable page 149 and ask them if they can identify the objects beginning with the **s** sound.

■ Make two copies of photocopiable page 149. Cut around the shapes and use them for games such as 'Snap' and 'Pairs'.

■ Ask the children to find the five differences in the second picture on photocopiable page 150.

■ Display photocopiable page 151. Ask the children to point to all the pictures of the snakes that they can see on the sheet.

THINKING

■ Ask the children to wriggle along the floor like a **snake**. Then encourage them to make very large snake **shapes** with their right hand and then with their left. Try this a few times, then try making snake shapes with two hands working together.

■ Ask the children to mime **swimming** on the floor using their arms and legs.

■ Invite the children to **skip** around in a circle. They should skip as fast as they can, without falling down. Ask them to try skipping with a rope. Ask two adults to hold each end of a rope for the children to jump over. How high can they jump? Teach them the words of any skipping **songs** that you know.

■ Ask the children to **stretch** their arms in the air, as high as they can. Now curl into a tiny ball. Stretch again, and curl up again into a tiny ball.

■ Use a set of mats to make a line of **stepping stones**. Ask the children to follow the path across them. Make the **spaces** between the stones wider and wider.

■ Together, make a game of **skittles** with plastic bottles filled with **sand**. Encourage the children to aim at the skittles with a ball or beanbag.

■ Encourage the children to imagine they are a **seed** in the ground. The **sun** comes out, and they begin to wake up and grow. They **slowly stretch** upwards until they are a big plant.

■ Ask the children to imagine they are a **sunflower**. They have a head full of **seeds**. Encourage them to walk around, **shaking** their heads to **spread** the seeds on the ground.

■ Invite the children to pretend they are **snails**, moving around very slowly and popping their heads in and out of their shells.

THINKING AND REASONING SKILLS

■ Show the children the picture on photocopiable page 148 and ask them the following questions:

1. Who is in the picture?
2. What is the weather like?
3. How do you know?
4. What is the girl going to do?
5. Is the girl there by herself?
6. Who else might be there?
7. What is the girl's name?
8. Is she on holiday?
9. Where do you think she is staying?
10. Have you been to the seaside?
11. What games did you play?
12. Why should you never throw sand?
13. How would you feel if someone threw sand at you?
14. What would you say and do?

Words beginning with *s*

Can you guess the words beginning with ***s***?

Answers: snake, scissors, sun, snail, snowman, star, spider, sandcastle

Spot the difference

Can you find five things that are different in the second picture?

Find the snakes

Point to the pictures of the snakes.

THE t SOUND

(t as in telephone)

PRONUNCIATION GUIDE

To make the **t** sound, open your mouth and put your tongue behind your top teeth. Move your tongue down, and feel the air coming out. There is no movement in the throat.

LISTENING

WHAT'S ON THE CD

- The rhymes and games for the t sound include:
  - Teddy Bear, Teddy Bear
  - Ten Little Men
  - Listening game

RHYMES AND SONGS

- Share rhymes and songs containing the **t** sound.

Tinker, Tailor, Soldier, Sailor

Tinker, tailor, soldier, sailor,
Rich man, poor man, beggar man,
Thief!

Tom, Tom the Piper's Son

Tom, Tom the piper's son,
Stole a pig and away he ran.
The pig was eat and Tom was beat,
And Tom went roaring down the street.

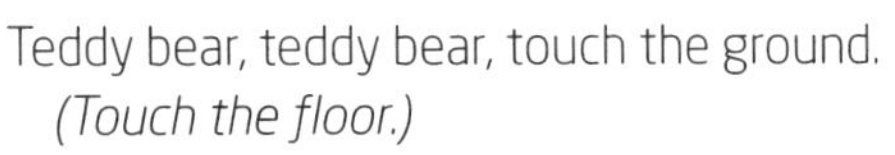

Teddy Bear, Teddy Bear

Teddy bear, teddy bear, touch the ground.
(Touch the floor.)
Teddy bear, teddy bear, turn around.
(Turn around.)
Teddy bear, teddy bear, go upstairs.
(Move legs up and down as though you are climbing stairs.)
Teddy bear, teddy bear, say your prayers.
(Put your hands together as though praying.)
Teddy bear, teddy bear, switch off the light.
(Jump up high to switch off the light.)
Teddy bear, teddy bear, say goodnight.
(Yawn and lie down and go to sleep.)

Little Tommy Tucker

Little Tommy Tucker sings for his supper,
What shall we give him? Brown bread and butter.
How shall he cut it without a knife?
How shall he marry without a wife?

I Have Two Eyes

I have two eyes to see with,
I have two feet to run,
I have two hands to wave with,
And nose I have but one.
I have two ears to hear with,
And a tongue to say 'Good day'.

Twinkle, Twinkle Little Star

Twinkle, twinkle little star, how I wonder what you are.
Up above the world so high, like a diamond in the sky.

When the blazing sun is gone, when he nothing shines upon,
Then you show your little light, twinkle, twinkle all the night.
Twinkle, twinkle little star, how I wonder what you are.

Then the traveller in the dark, thanks you for your tiny spark,
He could not see which way to go, if you did not twinkle so.
Twinkle, twinkle little star, how I wonder what you are.

In the dark blue sky you keep, and often through my curtains peep,
For you never shut your eye, 'till the sun is in the sky.
Twinkle, twinkle little star, how I wonder what you are.

As your bright and tiny spark lights the traveller in the dark,
Though I know not what you are – twinkle, twinkle, little star.
Twinkle, twinkle little star, how I wonder what you are.

Two Little Dicky Birds

Two little dicky birds sitting on a wall,
(Use your two index fingers.)
One named Peter, one named Paul.
(Waggle Peter and then waggle Paul.)
Fly away Peter, fly away Paul,
(Put Peter behind your back and then put Paul behind your back.)
Come back Peter, come back Paul!
(Bring Peter back and then bring Paul back.)

Ten Little Men

Ten little men standing straight,
(Ten fingers standing up.)
Ten little men open the gate,
(Touch your two thumbs and pull them apart.)
Ten little men all in a ring,
(Join your thumbs and first fingers to make a circle.)
Ten little men bow to the king,
(Bend your fingers up and down.)
Ten little men dance all day,
(Ten fingers move around.)
Ten little men hide away.
(Hide your ten fingers in two fists.)

Tweedledum and Tweedledee

Tweedledum and Tweedledee
Agreed to have a battle,
For Tweedledum said Tweedledee
Had spoiled his nice new rattle.
Just then flew by a monstrous crow,
As big as a tar-barrel,
Which frightened both the heroes so,
They quite forgot their quarrel.

ACTIVITIES

Listen to the CD and ask the children if they can guess the missing words .
- For breakfast I like to eat... and drink ... (**toast and tea**)
- At bedtime I like to sleep with my cuddly... (**teddy**)

- Play an action game: an adult whispers an action to the child, remembering to emphasise the **t** sound. The child then has to act it out. Other children then try to guess the action. This is difficult, so give help and clues, so that the child is successful. For example, actions could include:
  - **Telephone** a friend.
  - **Taste** a new food.
  - Show your **teeth**.
  - **Talk** to a friend.
  - **Tear** a piece of paper.
  - **Tie** a knot.
  - **Type** a letter.
  - **Touch** your **toes**.
- Look for story books which begin with the **t** sound and read them aloud to your class. For example:

Tickle Monster by Paul Rogers and Joanna Burroughes (Walker Books Ltd)
Thomas the Tank Engine and Friends by Revd W Awdry (Dean & Son)
The Tiger who Came to Tea by Judith Kerr (HarperCollins Children's Books)
The Enormous Turnip (Ladybird)
Twinkle, Twinkle, Chocolate Bar by John Foster (Oxford University Press)
Ten in the Bed by Penny Dale (Walker Books Ltd)
Terrible, Terrible Tiger by Colin Hawkins and Jacqui Hawkins (Walker Books Ltd)
Tom Thumb (Ladybird Favourite Tales and others)
The Town Mouse and the Country Mouse (Ladybird and others)
Titch books by Pat Hutchins (Red Fox)

- Look for non-fiction books in the library. You can find books about tigers, tanks, tortoises and toys.
- Find children's names beginning with the **t** sound, such as Tom, Taariq, Tamir, Tim, Theresa, Tamsin, Tracy, Tara.
- Use pictures from magazines and catalogues of things beginning with the **t** sound. Do any toys begin with **t**?
- Ask the children to look for **t** objects in their immediate environment, including cupboards at home and in the supermarket. Have they **tasted tomatoes, toast, tarts, toffee, tagliatelle, tuna, tacos, tortillas, treacle**?
- Ask the children to make a **tea** party for their dolls or friends. Ask the following questions: *How many cups, saucers and plates will you need on the table? What will you make for them to eat? What will you give them to drink? What games will you play?*
- Make an indoor garden. Give the children deep **trays**, and place a layer of small stones or gravel at the bottom. Put a layer of damp compost on top of the stones. Cut the **tops** from carrots, **turnips**, celery, leeks or potatoes and plant them in the compost.
- Talk about how important it is for the children to clean their **teeth** well, using a **toothbrush** and **toothpaste**.

EVALUATION

- These questions are intended to assess children's ability to hear the **t** sound. Ask them to rub the outside part of their ears before they start to listen.
- Read the following questions to the children:
  1. What sound is at the beginning of these words? table, teapot, tent, toast, teeth, television, tiger, tortoise, toys, toes
  2. In these groups of three words, which word begins with the **t** sound?
     a) tent, camping, home
     b) story, toy, sister
     c) ham, teddy, sit
     d) fun, tiger, dance
     e) jump, mud, tooth
     f) teacher, do, down
  3. Clap when you hear a word with the **t** sound at the beginning:
     teacher, tap, bake, ten, take, help, toy, teeth, sheet

EXTENSION ACTIVITY

- As a further challenge for children you can try 'Robot talk'. A list of suggested words is given below.
  - The adult says the word such as 'toy' and then says it in 'Robot talk' /t/oy/, sounding out the

individual sounds. Then repeat this.

■ The child then says the word, for example 'toy'. It may take a few tries to perfect the word.

■ The adult then says the sounds and claps each one, for example /t/oy/. Then the child joins in.

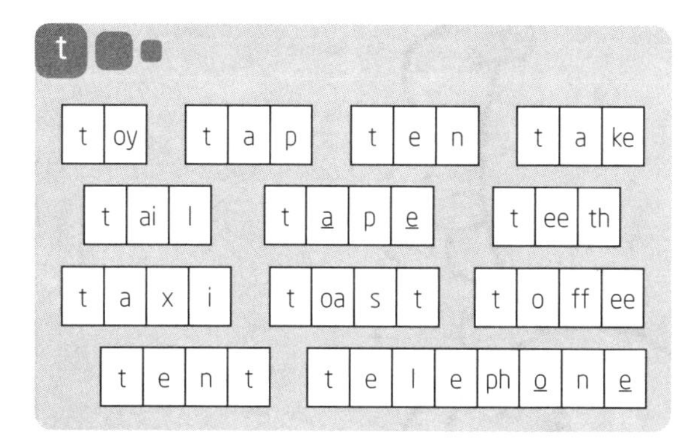

SEEING

■ Show the children photocopiable page 157 and ask them if they can identify the objects beginning with the **t** sound.

■ Make two copies of photocopiable page 157. Cut around the shapes and use them for games such as 'Snap' and 'Pairs'.

■ Show the children photocopiable page 158. Ask them if they can spot the five differences in the second picture on the sheet.

■ Display photocopiable page 159. Ask the children to help the teddy find his way to the picnic, either by tracing the route with a finger or drawing a line with a pencil. Encourage them to move their eyes from left to right as they complete the activity.

THINKING

■ Ask the children to **twist** their bodies around as far as they can. What can they see behind them?

■ Make a **tent** either indoors or outdoors using a blanket or a sheet. Invite the children to **take two toys** inside, curl up into a small ball and pretend to go to sleep.

■ Make a **training track**. Draw a very big chalk circle on the ground. Put out items on the circle that the children can jump over: ropes, skittles, a hoop. Time the children as they go right around the training track.

■ Ask the children to pretend that they have a heavy **teapot** in their hand. Try to pour out the **tea**. Take the teapot into their other hand. Remember that the teapot is very heavy! Pour out tea with the other hand. Try the first hand again, then swap again.

■ Ask the children to dance around, banging on a **tambourine**. Bang it high and bang it low.

■ Encourage the children to imagine they have a **telephone** in their hand (or let them use a toy telephone). Ask them to **talk** to their best friend on the phone, inviting him/her to come to their house to play. What toys will they play with?

■ Ask the children to imagine they are a **taxi**: moving around, **twisting** and **turning** to get through the **traffic**, **tooting** their horn to warn people that they are coming, remembering to charge money for the taxi ride. Do not bump into any other taxis!

■ Tell the children to imagine they are a slow, slow **tortoise**, crawling around the floor, looking for **tasty** grass to eat.

THINKING AND REASONING SKILLS

Show the children the picture on photocopiable page 156 and ask them the following questions:

1. Who is in the picture?
2. What is she doing?
3. What is she wearing?
4. Why is she dressed like this?
5. What is she carrying?
6. What do you do before you go to bed?
7. Do you like going to bed?
8. Do you take a toy to bed?
9. Why do we have to go to sleep?
10. Do you like bedtime stories?
11. What is your favourite story?
12. Do you dream at night?
13. What do you dream about?

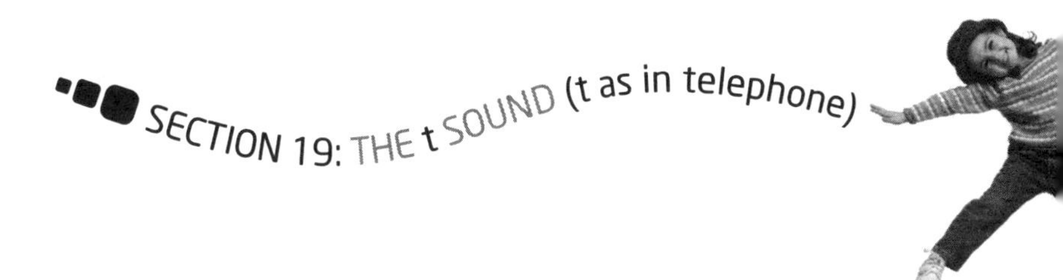

Words beginning with *t*

Can you guess the word beginning with ***t***?

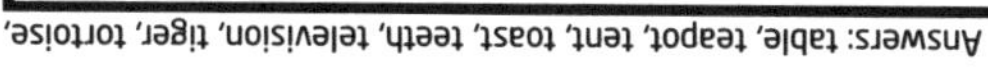

Answers: table, teapot, tent, toast, teeth, television, tiger, tortoise.

Spot the difference

Can you find five things that are different in the second picture?

Help Teddy

Help teddy find his way to the teddy bears' picnic.

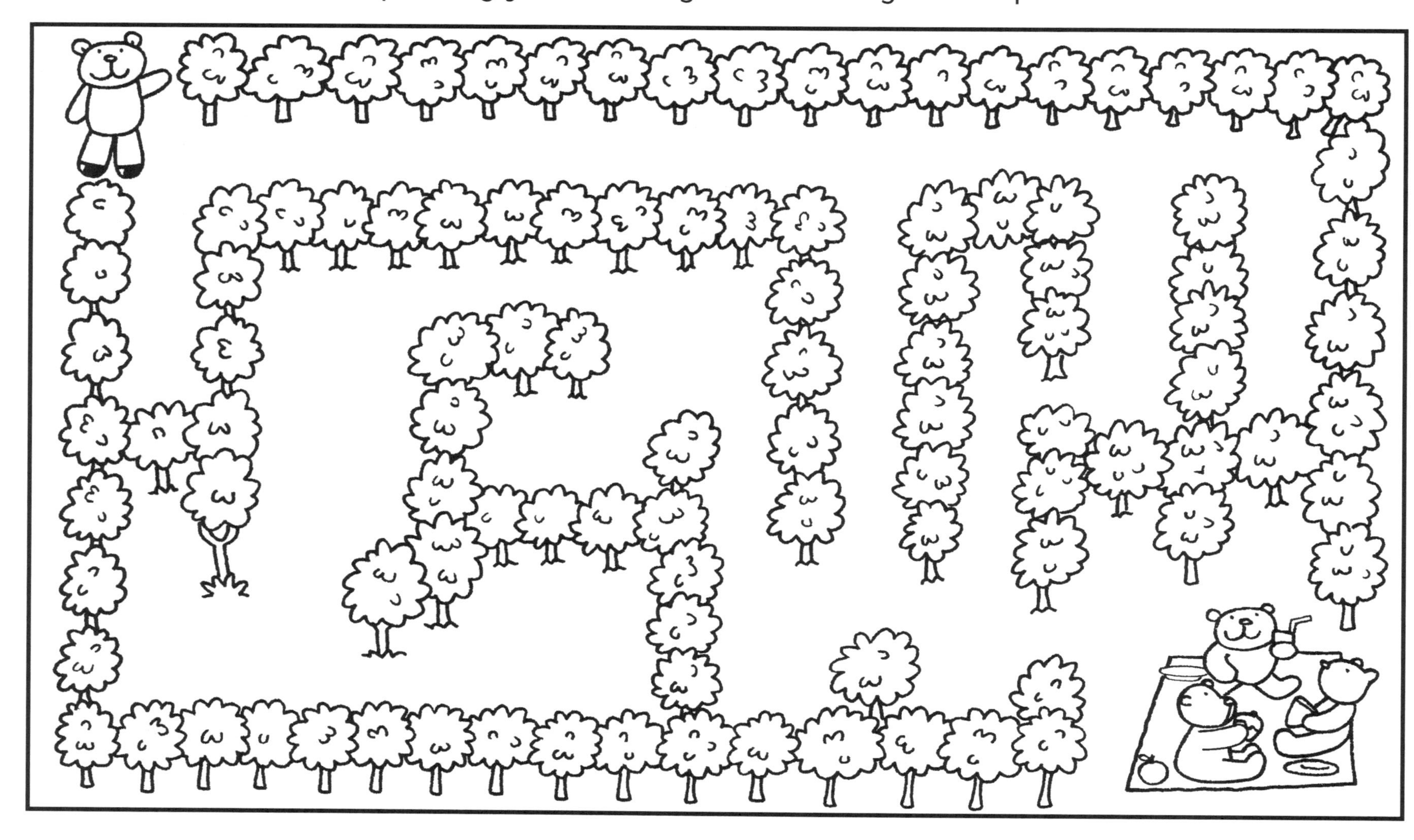

THE u SOUND

(u as in umbrella)

PRONUNCIATION GUIDE

To make the **u** sound, open your mouth a little, and make the sound at the back of your mouth. Some air comes out.

LISTENING

WHAT'S ON THE CD

- The rhymes and games for the **u** sound include:
  - Uncle Moon
  - Listening game

RHYMES AND SONGS

- Share rhymes and songs containing the **u** sound.

Upstairs, Downstairs

Upstairs, downstairs
Upon my lady's window,
There I saw a cup of sack
And a race of ginger.

Apples at the fire
And nuts to crack,
And a little boy in the cream pot,
Up to his neck.

Up at Piccadilly, Oh!

Up at Piccadilly, oh!
The coachman takes his stand,
And when he meets a pretty girl,
He takes her by the hand;
Whip away forever, oh!
Drive away so clever, oh!
All the way to Bristol, oh!
He drives her four-in-hand.

Rub-a-Dub-Dub

Rub-a-dub-dub
Three men in a tub,
And who do you think they be?
The butcher, the baker,
The candlestick maker,
Turn 'em out, knaves all three

Up the Wooden Hill

Up the wooden hill
To Bedfordshire,
Down Sheet Lane
To Blanket Fair.

See a Pin and Pick it Up

See a pin and pick it up,
All the day you'll have good luck;
See a pin and let it lay,
Bad luck you'll have all the day.

Gee up Neddy to the Fair

Gee up Neddy to the fair
What shall we buy when we get there?
A penny apple or a penny pear
What shall we buy when we get there!

Uncle Moon

Uncle Moon! Uncle Moon!
I am going to Dehradoon.
If you come by here soon,
I will give you a red balloon.

There Was an Old Woman Tossed Up in a Basket

There was an old woman tossed up in a basket
Ninety-nine times as high as the moon.
What she did there I could not but ask it
For in each hand she carried a broom.

'Old woman, old woman, old woman,' said I
'Where are you going to up so high?'
'To sweep the cobwebs from the sky
And you may come with me if you can fly.'

Goosey, Goosey, Gander

Goosey, goosey, gander
Whither shall I wander?
Upstairs and downstairs and in my lady's chamber.
There I met an old man
Who wouldn't say his prayers,
I took him by the left leg
And threw him down the stairs.

ACTIVITIES

Listen to the CD and ask the children if they can guess the missing word in the sentence. The sentence and answer is below.

- When it rains I like to put up my... **(umbrella)**

■ Find a straw, and blow air through it to make bubbles under the water. Then put a small drop of washing-up liquid in the water. Blow again. What happens now **under** the water? (If the children try this, make sure they do not suck up the water.)

■ Play an action game: an adult whispers an action to the child, remembering to emphasise the **u** sound. The child then has to act it out. Other children then try to guess the action. This is difficult, so give help and clues, so that the child is successful. For example, actions could include:

- Climb **up**.
- Go **under** the table.
- Go **upstairs**.
- **Undo** shoe laces.
- **Unwrap** a present.
- Put up an **umbrella**.
- Turn something **upside down**.

■ Look for story books which begin with the **u** sound and read them aloud to your class. For example:

The Ugly Duckling (Ladybird Tales)
Under the Moon and over the Sea by John Agard, Grace Nichols, Cathie Felstead and Jane Rae (Walker Books Ltd)
Up and up by Shirley Hughes (Red Fox)
The Umbrella by Jan Brett (Putnam Publishing Group)

■ Look for non-fiction books in the library. You can find books about underwater creatures, or animals that live underground.

■ Find children's names beginning with the **u** sound, for example, Unwin, Usher, Uqbah, Ursula.

■ Slice open an **onion**. Ask the children to look at all the layers inside. Tell them that the layers contain food that help the plant grow. Put an onion in a dark place. Watch the roots grow, then the green plant.

■ If you have a doll's house at your setting, talk about what you would expect to find in the rooms **upstairs**.

■ Put a small object inside a small box. Wrap the box in lots of layers of paper or newspaper. Give the box to one of the children and watch them **unwrap** all the layers. You could also play 'Pass the parcel', with the children unwrapping a layer of paper every time the music stops.

EVALUATION

■ These questions are intended to assess children's ability to hear the **u** sound. Ask them to rub the outside part of their ears before they start to listen.

■ Read the following questions to the children:

1. What sound is at the beginning of these words?
   umbrella, uncle, up, underground, upside down, underwater, unhappy, upset
2. In these groups of three words, which word begins with the **u** sound?
   a) up, down, town
   b) rain, sun, umbrella
   c) beach, uncle, run
   d) doll, tree, unhappy,
   e) moon, upset, animal
   f) jam, market, upstairs
3. Clap when you hear a word with the **u** sound at the beginning:
   umbrella, uncle, up, foot, underground, underwater, tree, unhappy, upset

EXTENSION ACTIVITY

■ As a further challenge for children you can try 'Robot talk'. A list of suggested words is given below.

- The adult says the word such as 'up' and then says it in 'Robot talk' /u/p/, sounding out the individual sounds. Then repeat this.

■ The child then says the word, for example 'up'. It may take a few tries to perfect the word.
■ The adult then says the sounds and claps each one, for example /u/p/. Then the child joins in.

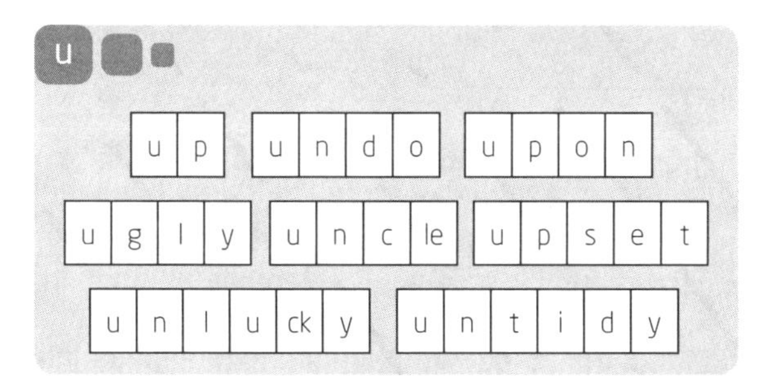

SEEING

■ Show the children photocopiable page 165 and ask them if they can identify the objects beginning with the **u** sound.
■ Make two copies of photocopiable page 165. Cut around the shapes and use them for games such as 'Snap' and 'Pairs'.
■ Ask the children to join up the pairs of matching umbrellas on photocopiable page 166, either by tracing lines with a finger or using a pencil.
■ Ask the children to join the dots to make a picture of an umbrella on photocopiable page 167.

THINKING

■ Ask the children to pretend they are a rabbit, living **underground**. Tell them to pop **up** and down from their rabbit hole, and hop around.
■ Tell the children to pull their arms and legs in like a folded **umbrella**. Imagine someone is opening them up. They should jump up, with their arms out wide. (Show the children a folded and an open umbrella.)
■ Ask the children to imagine they are a clown, walking along a tightrope in a circus. They have an opened **umbrella**. Draw a line on the ground. Invite the children to walk along it, keeping their balance while holding their umbrella **up** in the air.
■ Ask the children to throw a ball or beanbag **up** in the air. They should throw it a little way up at first, and see if they can catch it. Then encourage them to try throwing it a bit higher. How high can they throw it and catch it?
■ Tell the children the story of the **Ugly** Duckling. Ask them to imagine they are the duckling.
■ How do they feel when the other birds don't want to play with them? Are they **unhappy**? Are they lonely? Are they **upset**?
■ How do they feel when they become swans?
■ Act out the story, doing actions for the duckling and the swan.
■ Talk about how the children feel when they have no one to play with. Ask: *Has anyone told you that you cannot play with them? How did you feel? Were you angry,* ***unhappy****, sad? Did you find another friend to play with?*

THINKING AND REASONING SKILLS

■ Show the children the picture on photocopiable page 164 and ask them the following questions:
1. Who is in the picture?
2. What is he doing?
3. Why is it hard to put up the umbrella?
4. What do you think will happen to the umbrella?
5. What is an umbrella made from?
6. Why does the rainwater not come through the cloth?
7. What clothes do you wear in wet weather?
8. Does the rainwater come through the clothes and make you wet?
9. What would happen if we had no rain?
10. What happens in countries that have hardly any rain?
11. What do plants need to grow?

Words beginning with *u*

Can you guess the word beginning with ***u***?

Answers: umbrella, upstairs, upside down, underwater, unhappy, unwrap, onion, oven

Match the umbrellas

Draw a line to match the umbrellas that are the same.

Dot-to-dot umbrella

Join up the dots to make an umbrella.

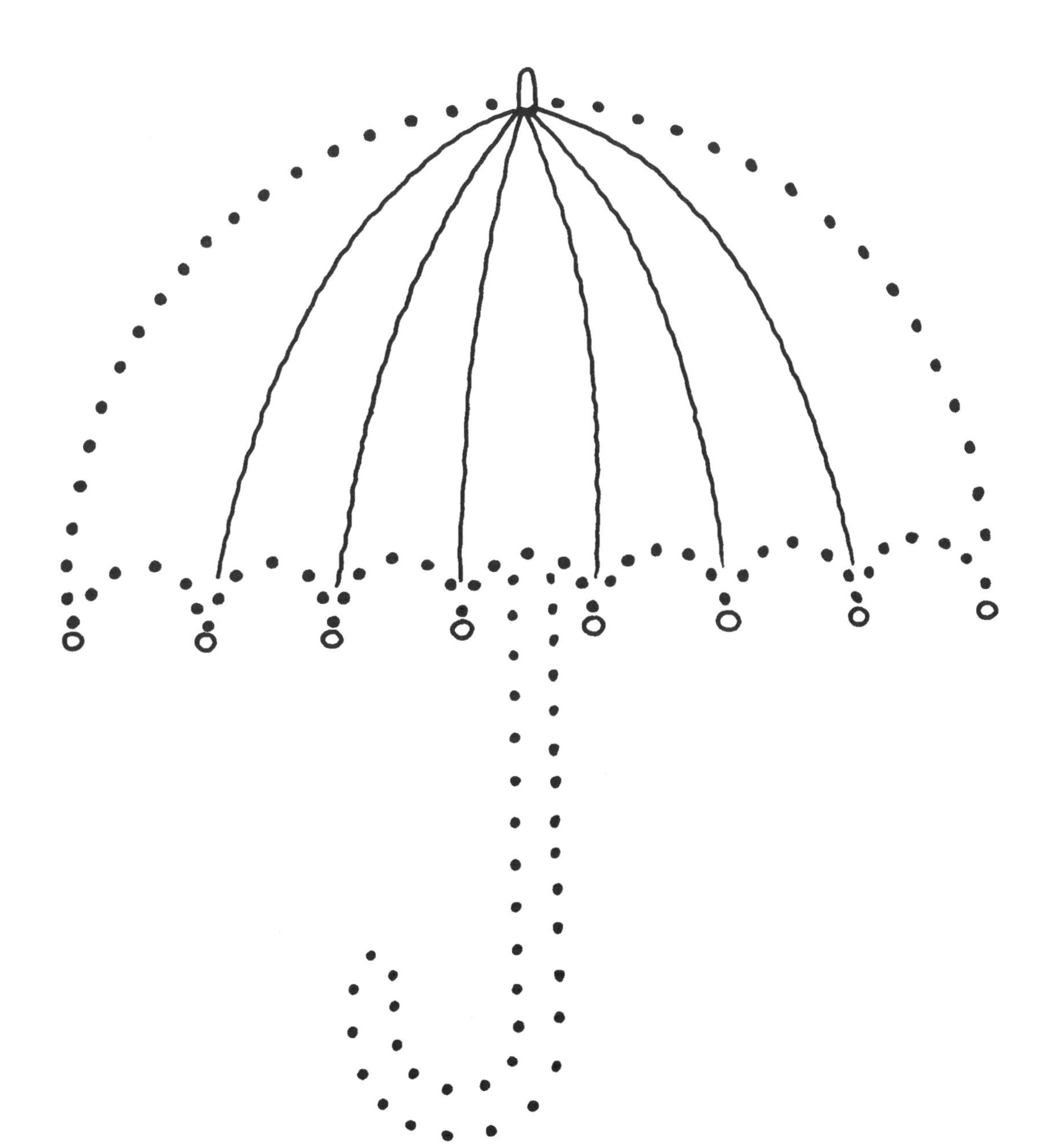

THE v SOUND

(v as in van)

PRONUNCIATION GUIDE

To make the **v** sound, put your top teeth on top of your bottom lip. Push air through your teeth. We make the sound at the back of the throat. Feel your throat and your lips vibrate.

LISTENING

WHAT'S ON THE CD

- The rhymes and games for the v sound include:
  - Roses are Red
  - Listening game

RHYMES AND SONGS

- Share rhymes and songs containing the **v** sound.

V is for Vulture

V is for Vulture
That feeds on things dead.
It would probably rather
Eat pancakes instead!

As I was going to St Ives

As I was going to St Ives,
I met a man with seven wives,
Each wife had seven sacks,
Each sack had seven cats,
Each cat had seven kits;
Kits, cats, sacks and wives;
How many were there going to St Ives?

NB: the **v** sound is not in the initial position in this rhyme, but it provides good practice of the sound.

Roses are Red

Roses are red,
Violets are blue,
Sugar is sweet,
And so are you.

Vintery, Mintery, Cutery, Corn

Vintery, mintery, cutery, corn,
Apple seed and apple thorn;
Wire, briar, limber lock,
Three geese in a flock.
One flew east,
And one flew west,
And one flew over the cuckoo's nest.

One, Two, Three, Four, Five

One, two, three, four, five,
Once I caught a fish alive.
Six, seven, eight, nine, ten,
Then I let it go again.
Why did you let it go?
Because it bit my finger so.
Which finger did it bite?
This little finger on the right.

One, Two, Buckle My Shoe

One, two,
Buckle my shoe;
Three, four,
Knock at the door;
Five, six,
Pick up sticks;
Seven, eight,
Lay them straight;
Nine, ten,
A good, fat hen;
Eleven, twelve,
Dig and delve;
Thirteen, fourteen,
Maids a-courting;
Fifteen, sixteen,
Maids in the kitchen;
Seventeen, eighteen,
Maids a-waiting;
Nineteen, twenty,
My plate's empty.

Salt, Mustard, Vinegar, Pepper

Skipping rhyme

Salt, mustard,
Vinegar, pepper,
Rich man, poor man,
Beggar man, thief!

ACTIVITIES

Listen to the CD and ask the children if they can guess what the sound effects are. Questions and answers are below.
- What is the boy using to clean the carpet? **(vacuum cleaner)**
- What instrument is being played? **(violin)**

- Play an action game: an adult whispers an action to the child, remembering to emphasise the **v** sound. The child then has to act it out. Other children then try to guess the action. This is difficult, so give help and clues, so that the child is successful. For example, actions could include:
  - Make something **vanish**.
  - **Visit** a friend.
  - Sniff a **violet**.
  - Pretend to play the **violin**.
  - Put on your **vest**.
  - Use the **vacuum** cleaner.
- Look for story books which begin with the **v** sound and read them aloud to your class. For example:

The Very Hungry Caterpillar by Eric Carle (Puffin Books)
The Very Quiet Cricket by Eric Carle (Philomel Books)
The Very Kind Rich Lady and Her One Hundred Dogs by Chinlun Lee (Walker Books Ltd)

- Look for non-fiction books in the library. You can find books about volcanoes, vultures, vans, vegetables and violins.
- Find children's names beginning with the **v** sound, such as Victor, Varinder, Valerie, Vera, Varda.
- Make a scrap book, using pictures of **vegetables** cut out of magazines.
- Ask the children to name some of the **vegetables** that they like. Look in cookery books to find vegetable soups to make. Make vegetable soup together (an adult will have to do most of this). (Ensure that you are aware of any food allergies or dietary requirements before commencing this activity.)
- Ask the children whether they have tasted **vanilla** ice cream or **vinegar** on fish and chips. Discuss the differences in the flavours.

EVALUATION

- These questions are intended to assess the children's ability to hear the **v** sound. Ask them to rub the outside part of their ears before they start to listen.
- Read the following questions to the children:
  1. What sound is at the beginning of these words?
     van, vegetables, volcano, vase, violin, vest, violet, vinegar, vet
  2. In these groups of three words, which word begins with the **v** sound?
     a) vet, wet, pet
     b) talk, good, vase
     c) thin, violin, went
     d) village, dress, card
     e) farm, hens, visit
     f) tank, volcano, fish
  3. Clap when you hear a word with a **v** sound at the beginning:
     thin, vest, violet, vinegar, vet, fish, vegetables, volcano, vase

EXTENSION ACTIVITY

- As a further challenge for children you can try 'Robot talk'. A list of suggested words is given below.
  - The adult says the word such as 'van' and then says it in 'Robot talk' /v/a/n/, sounding out the

individual sounds. Then repeat this.

■ The child then says the word, for example 'van'. It may take a few tries to perfect the word.

■ The adult then says the sounds and claps each one, for example /v/a/n/. Then the child joins in.

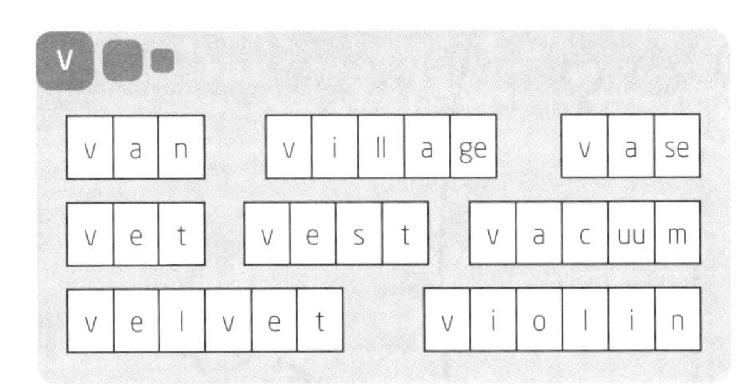

SEEING

■ Show the children photocopiable page 173 and ask them if they can identify the objects beginning with the **v** sound.

■ Make two copies of photocopiable page 173. Cut around the shapes and use them for games such as 'Snap' and 'Pairs'.

■ Ask the children to find the five differences in the second picture on photocopiable page 174.

■ Display photocopiable page 175. Ask the children to match up the pairs of vases, either by tracing a line with a finger, or using a pencil.

THINKING

■ Ask the children to curl into a tiny ball, then jump up and explode like a **volcano**. Tell them to stretch out their arms and legs as they jump, making a **very** big shape. Encourage them to hiss as they jump up, like the steam in the volcano. Together, look at some photographs of volcanoes.

■ Invite the children to run around the playground, pretending they are driving a **van**. Tell them to weave in and out of the traffic as they are in a hurry (but be careful not to bump into anyone!), tooting their horn **very** loudly, slowing down at the traffic lights, then going fast again.

■ Play a recording of some **violin** music (for example, violin concertos by Tchaikovsky, Beethoven or Prokofiev). Ask the children to pretend to play the violin in an orchestra, using the bow to go across the strings, and using their fingers to touch the strings at the top of the violin.

■ Tell the children to imagine that they are a **vet**. They are looking after a little kitten that is ill – giving it some medicine, and then stroking it gently, enjoying the soft, **velvety** fur. Encourage the children to keep stroking the tiny kitten, until it falls asleep in their arms.

THINKING AND REASONING SKILLS

■ Show the children the picture on photocopiable page 172 and ask them the following questions:

1. What is in the picture?
2. What might happen to the vase?
3. What is in the vase?
4. Do you think the vase will break? Why?
5. Who will clean up the flowers and the water?
6. What kind of vase will not break if it falls?
7. What will happen to the flowers if they are left out of water?
8. How will the person, who left the vase at the edge of the table, feel?
9. Will they be happy or sad?
10. Have you ever broken anything at home?
11. What was it?
12. What did you say? What did you do?
13. Who did it belong to?
14. What did they say? What did they do?

Words beginning with *v*

Can you guess the word beginning with ***v***?

Answers: van, vegetables, volcano, vase, violin, vacuum cleaner, vest, vet

Spot the difference

Can you find five things that are different in the second picture?

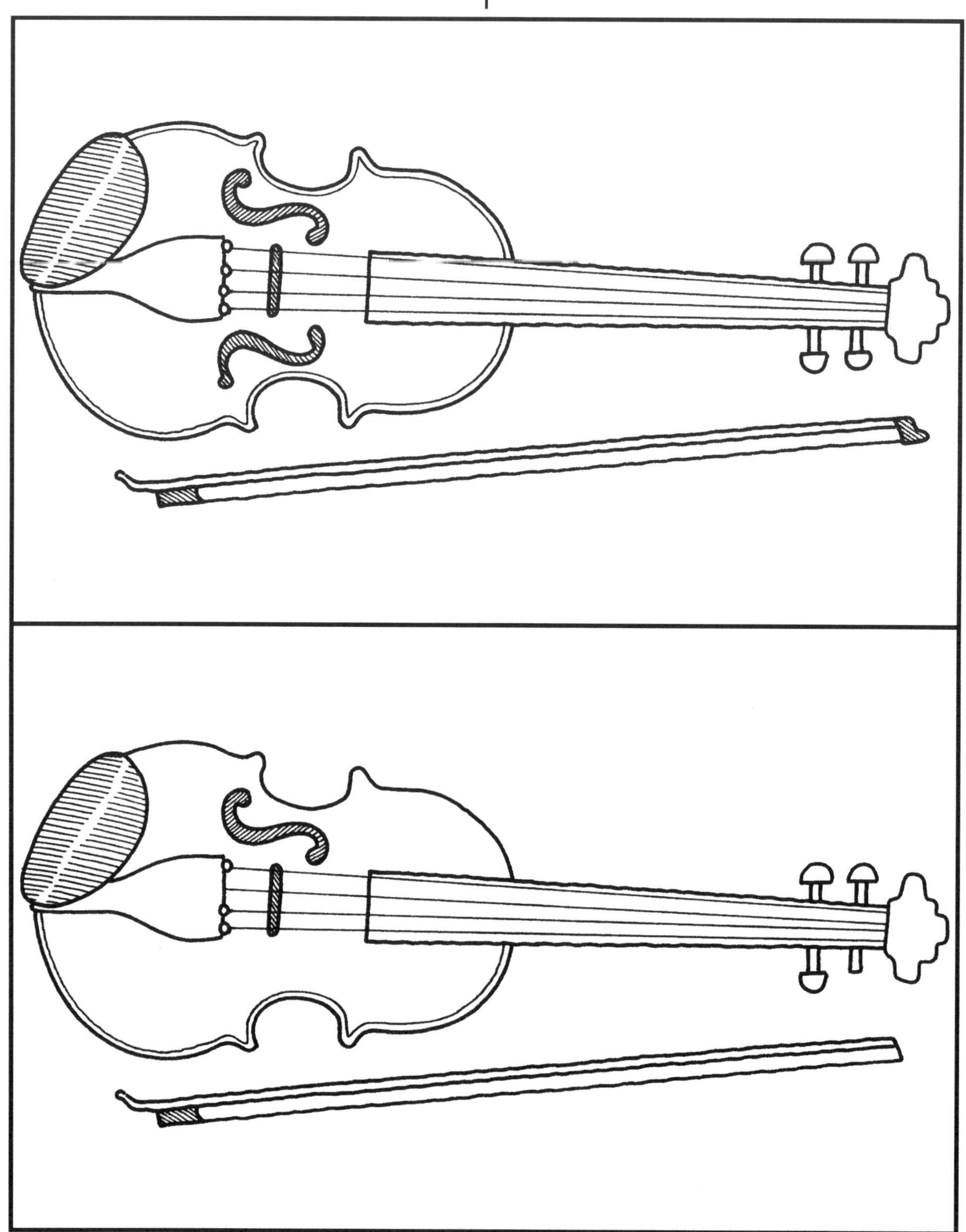

Matching game

Can you match the vases that are the same?

THE w SOUND

(w as in window, o as in one)

PRONUNCIATION GUIDE
To make the **w** sound, form your lips into a small circle, then open them up again, and let out air. The sound is made at the back of the throat.

LISTENING

WHAT'S ON THE CD

- The rhymes and games for the w sound include:
  - Incy Wincy Spider
  - Listening game

RHYMES AND SONGS

- Share rhymes and songs containing the **w** sound.

The Worm Song

Nobody likes me,
Ev'rybody hates me,
Guess I'll go eat worms.
Long, thin, slimy ones,
Short, fat, juicy ones,
Itsy, bitsy, fuzzy, wuzzy worms.

Down goes the first one,
Down goes the second one,
Oh, how they wiggle and squirm.
Long, thin, slimy ones,
Short, fat, juicy ones,
Itsy, bitsy, fuzzy, wuzzy worms.

Up comes the first one,
Up comes the second one,
Oh, how they wiggle and squirm.
Long, thin, slimy ones,
Short, fat, juicy ones,
Itsy, bitsy, fuzzy, wuzzy worms.

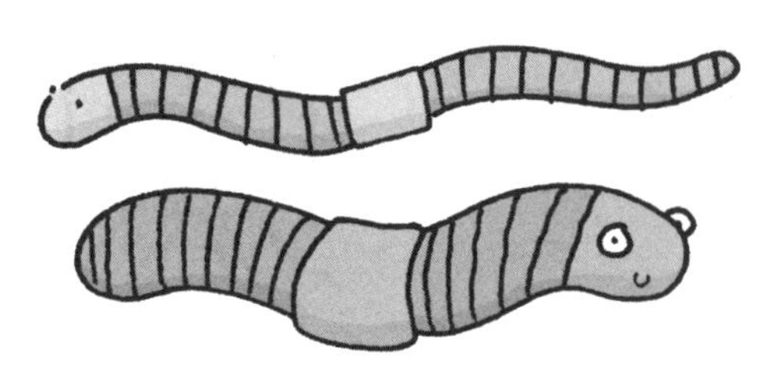

Marching in our Wellingtons

We're marching in our Wellingtons;
Tramp, tramp, tramp,
We're marching in our Wellingtons,
We won't get damp.
We're marching in our Wellingtons;
Stamp, stamp, stamp.
We're marching in our Wellingtons,
We won't get damp.

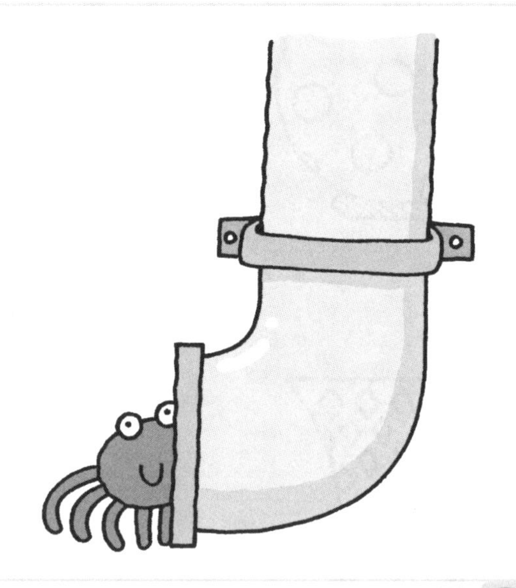

Incy Wincy Spider

Incy wincy spider
Climbing up the spout;
Down came the rain
And washed the spider out:
Out came the sun
And dried up all the rain;
Incy wincy spider
Climbing up again.

Wiggly Woo

There's a worm at the bottom of the garden,
And his name is Wiggly Woo.
There's a worm at the bottom of the garden,
And all that he can do,
Is wiggle all night, and wiggle all day.
The people round here, they all do say,
There's a worm at the bottom of the garden,
And his name is Wiggly,
Wig, wig, wiggly Woo.

Way Down South where Bananas Grow

Way down south where bananas grow,
A grasshopper stood on an elephant's toe.
The elephant said, with tears in his eyes,
'Pick on somebody your own size.'

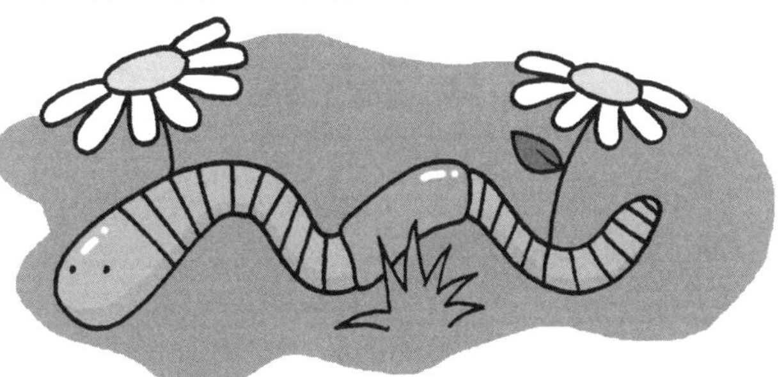

From Wibbleton to Wobbleton

From Wibbleton to Wobbleton is fifteen miles.
From Wobbleton to Wibbleton is fifteen miles.
From Wibbleton to Wobbleton,
From Wobbleton to Wibbleton
Is fifteen miles.

This is the Way we Wash our Hands

This is the way we wash our hands,
Wash our hands, wash our hands.
This is the way we wash our hands
On a cold and frosty morning.
This is the way we....

Wash our faces...

Clean our nails...

Brush our teeth...

Comb our hair...

Give a hug...

Actions
Stand in a circle and perform each action in each verse.

Wee Willie Winkie

Wee Willie Winkie runs through the town,
Upstairs and downstairs in his nightgown,
Tapping at the window and crying through the lock,
'Are all the children in their beds? It's past eight o'clock.'

ACTIVITIES

Listen to the CD and ask the children if they can guess what the sound effects are. Questions and answers are below.

- What is the weather like outside? **(windy)**
- What is the person doing? **(walking)**
- What is the noise? **(whistling)**

■ Play an action game: an adult whispers an action to the child, remembering to emphasise the **w** sound. The child then has to act it out. Other children then try to guess the action. This is difficult, so give help and clues, so that the child is successful. For example, actions could include:

- **Wake** up.
- **Walk** around.
- **Wash** your face.
- **Wave** your hand.
- **Wear** a coat.
- **Water** the plants.
- **Weed** the garden.
- **Weigh** a parcel at the post office.

■ Look for story books which begin with the **w** sound and read them aloud to your class. For example:

The Wonderful Wizard of Oz by L Frank Baum (Penguin)
We're Going on a Bear Hunt by Michael Rosen (Walker Books Ltd)
Where's Wally? by Martin Handford (Walker Books Ltd)
Wombat Goes Walkabout by Michael Morpurgo and Christian Birmingham (Picture Lions)
Winnie the Witch by Valerie Thomas and Korky Paul (Oxford University Press)
Peter and the Wolf (Ladybird and others)
Mr Wolf's Week by Colin Hawkins (Mammoth)

■ Look for non-fiction books in the library. You can find books about the weather, watches and windmills.

■ Find children's names beginning with the **w** sound, such as William, Waseem, Willow, Wilma, Waheeba.

■ Fill a bowl with **water**. Ask the children to find things that float. Show them how to make a small boat shape from aluminium foil and then sail it. Encourage them to try to float things like a metal spoon or a metal coin. Ask them if the objects float, and if they can work out why/why not.

■ Ask the children if they know why they **wash** their hands after using the toilet and before touching food.

■ Give the children a set of scales to **weigh** different things, making sure that they understand how the scales **work**. Ask them to find small and large objects to weigh. Ask: *Will the large objects always be heavier than the small ones?* Get them to hold different items in their hands, and say if they are heavy or light. Encourage them to guess first before they actually pick up the items.

EVALUATION

■ These questions are intended to assess children's ability to hear the **w** sound. Ask them to rub the outside part of their ears before they start to listen.

■ Read the following questions to the children:

1. What sound is at the beginning of these words? watch, window, windmill, wall, web, wigwam
2. In these groups of three words, which word begins with the **w** sound?
   a) wig, think, school
   b) sun, wind, rain
   c) window, friend, open
   d) nip, wasp, tin
   e) teacher, book, water
   f) vase, new, watch
3. Clap when you hear a word with the **w** sound at the beginning:
   web, wigwam, bird, worm, wasp, friend, watch, sun

EXTENSION ACTIVITY

■ As a further challenge for children you can try 'Robot talk'. A list of suggested words is given below.

■ The adult says the word such as 'wig' and then says it in 'Robot talk' /w/i/g/, sounding out the individual sounds. Then repeat this.

■ The child then says the word, for example 'wig'. It may take a few tries to perfect the word.

■ The adult then says the sounds and claps each one, for example /w/i/g/. Then the child joins in.

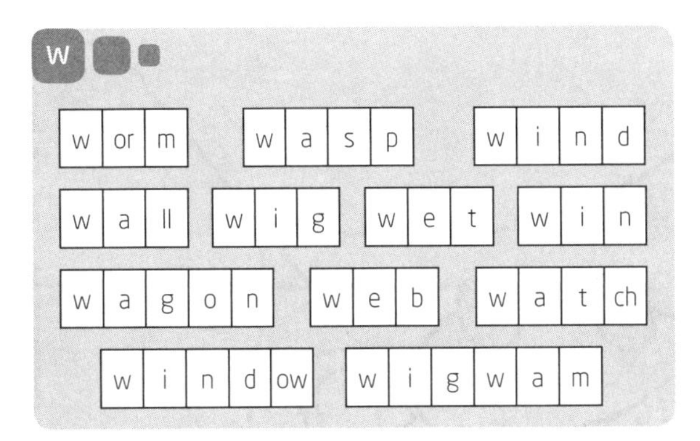

SEEING

■ Show the children photocopiable page 181 and ask them if they can identify the objects beginning with the **w** sound.

■ Make two copies of photocopiable page 181. Cut around the shapes and use them for games such as 'Snap' and 'Pairs'.

■ Display photocopiable page182. Ask the children to point to the four watches in the array of items on the page.

■ Ask the children to help the spider to its web on photocopiable page 183. They could trace the path with their finger or use a pencil. Encourage them to move their eyes from left to right as they complete the activity.

THINKING

■ Draw a straight line along the ground. Ask the children to first **walk** along the line, then run, hop, skip or twirl along it. They must try to stay on the line each time.

■ Invite the children to try **walking** on their tiptoes, then walking on their heels. Walk on the insides of their feet, now walk on the outsides of their feet.

■ Encourage the children to imagine they are a **windmill**, making their arms go round like a windmill. At first there is a strong wind, but then the wind stops. What happens to their arms? Suddenly the wind begins again.

■ What happens inside a **windmill**? Say the rhyme:

Blow wind, blow
And go, mill, go.
That the miller
May grind his corn;
That the baker may take it,
And into rolls make it
And bring us some
Hot in the morn.

■ Tell the children to imagine they are going to a **wedding**. What will they **wear**? They should put on their very best clothes. How will they travel to the wedding? What will happen there? Who will be there? What will they eat? Have they ever been to a wedding? Find pictures of weddings in magazines.

THINKING AND REASONING SKILLS

■ Show the children the picture on photocopiable page 180 and ask them the following questions:

1. What two creatures are in the picture?
2. What is the spider doing?
3. What is the fly doing?
4. Why is the spider sitting in the web?
5. How many legs does the spider have?
6. How many legs has the fly?
7. What happens to the fly if it gets caught in the web?
8. How does a spider spin its web?
9. Are all spider webs the same shape?
10. How often do spiders make a new web?

Words beginning with *w*

Can you guess the word beginning with ***w***?

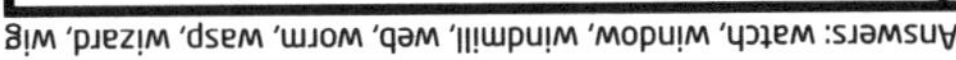

Find the watches

Point to the watches on the page.

Help the spider

Help the spider reach its web along the branches of the tree.

THE x SOUND

(x as in **fox**)

PRONUNCIATION GUIDE
To make the **x** sound, put your tongue behind your bottom teeth. Move your tongue forward a little. Push the air out. Make the sound at the front of your mouth through your teeth.

LISTENING

WHAT'S ON THE CD

- The rhymes and games for the x sound include:
  - Foxy's Hole
  - Listening game

RHYMES AND SONGS

- Share rhymes and songs containing the **x** sound.

Foxy's Hole
Finger play

Put your finger in foxy's hole
(Make a circle with a finger and thumb, and 'look in' with index finger of other hand.)
Foxy's not at home.
Foxy's out at the back door,
Picking at a bone.
(Push finger right through the hole and wriggle it around.)

Sing a Song of Sixpence

Sing a song of sixpence, a pocket full of rye,
Four and twenty blackbirds baked in a pie.
When the pie was opened, the birds began to sing,
Was not that a dainty dish to set before the king?

The king was in his counting-house, counting out his money,
The queen was in the parlour, eating bread and honey,
The maid was in the garden, hanging out the clothes,
Along came a blackbird and snapped off her nose.

Multiplication Is Vexation

Multiplication is vexation,
Division is as bad;
Rule of Three doth puzzle me,
And Practice drives me mad.

X as in Fox

X as in fox
That hunts in the night
And can hear any noise,
No matter how slight.

Six Little Mice

Six little mice sat down to spin;
Pussy passed by and she peeped in;
'What are you doing, my little men?'
'Weaving coats for gentlemen.'
'Shall I come in and cut off your threads?'
'No, no, Mistress Pussy, you'd bite off our heads.'
'Oh, no, I'll not; I'll help you to spin.'
'That may be so, but you can't come in!'

Mix a Pancake

Mix a pancake,
(Vigorously beat the batter in a pretend bowl.)
Stir a pancake,
(Stir the mixture slowly.)
Pop it in the pan;
(Put a spoonful in the frying pan.)
Fry a pancake,
(Move the frying pan around gently.)
Toss a pancake –
(Toss the pancake up in the air.)
Catch it if you can.
(Run to catch the pancake.)

If All the Seas Were One Sea

If all the seas were one sea,
What a great sea that would be!
And if all the trees were one tree,
What a great tree that would be!
And if all the axes were one axe,
What a great axe that would be!
And if all the men were one man,
What a great man he would be!
And if the great man took the great axe,
And cut down the great tree,
And let it fall into the great sea,
What a splish splash that would be!

A Hunting We Will Go

A hunting we will go,
A hunting we will go,
We'll catch a fox
And put him in a box
And then we'll let him go.

SECTION 23: THE x SOUND (x as in fox)

ACTIVITIES

Listen to the CD and ask the children if they can guess the missing words in the sentences. The sentences and answers are below.

- Guess what I am. I have red fur, a big bushy tail and I wake at nightime. (**fox**)
- In the morning I put on my shoes and... before going to school. (**socks**)
- At the end of the day I put all my toys in the toy... (**box**)

- Play an action game: an adult whispers an action to the child, remembering to emphasise the **x** sound. The child then has to act it out. Other children then try to guess the action. This is difficult, so give help and clues, so that the child is successful. For example, actions could include:
  - Stir a cake **mixture**.
  - Chop wood with an **axe**.
  - Wave for a **taxi**.
  - Point to an **exit** from the room.
  - **Explore** a jungle.
  - Hold up **six** fingers.
  - Be a Jack-in-the-**box**.
- Look for story books which contain words with the **x** sound and read them aloud to your class. For example:

Father Fox's Christmas Rhymes by Clyde Watson and Wendy Watson (Square Fish)
The Fox and the Hound (Grolier Books, Disney)
Fantastic Mr Fox by Roald Dahl (Puffin Books)
Fox in Socks by Dr Seuss (Picture Lions)
The Sly Fox and the Hen (Ladybird and others)
A Fox Got my Socks by Hilda Offen (Red Fox)

- Look for non-fiction books in the library. You can find books about foxes, explorers, bees and wax.
- Find children's names containing the **x** sound, such as Rex, Maxine, Dixie, Alexis.
- Collect **boxes** of different shapes and sizes. Ask the children if they can make a house or a fort with the boxes. Encourage them to make an ambulance or a **taxi** with a box. Show them how to cut out circles for wheels (or collect round cheese boxes for wheels).
- Encourage the children to make a tea party for **six** friends. Ask them to count out six mugs (or six cups and saucers), six plates, six spoons, six pieces of fruit or six snacks.

EVALUATION

- These questions are intended to assess the children's ability to hear the **x** sound. Ask them to rub the outside part of their ears before they start to listen.
- Read the following questions to the children:

1. What sound is in all of these words?
   taxi, box, fox, explosion, six
2. In the following groups of three words, which word contains the **x** sound?
   a) mix, hat, coat
   b) pick, fox, witch
   c) zip, taxi, hold
   d) dart, mug, axe
   e) box, cold, nose
   f) cup, plate, six
3. Clap when you hear a word with the **x** sound in it:
   box, fox, axe, cup, six, sixty, sixteen, doctor

EXTENSION ACTIVITY

- As a further challenge for children you can try 'Robot talk'. A list of suggested words is given below.
  - The adult says the word such as 'box' and then says it in 'Robot talk' /b/o/x/, sounding out the individual sounds. Then repeat this.
  - The child then says the word, for example 'box'.

It may take a few tries to perfect the word.

■ The adult then says the sounds and claps each one, for example /b/o/x/. Then the child joins in.

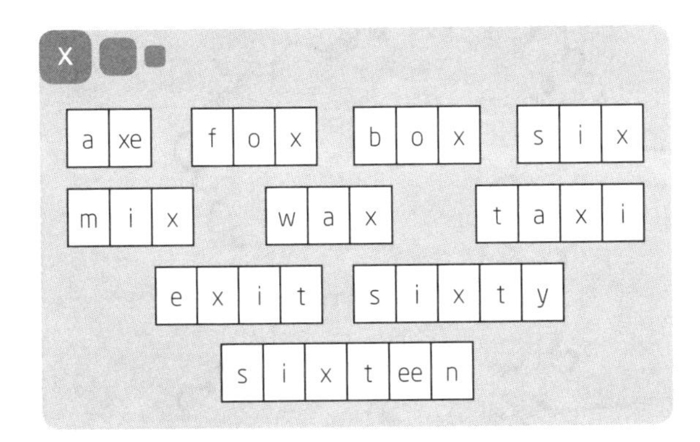

SEEING

■ Show the children photocopiable page 189 and ask them if they can identify the objects containing the **x** sound.

■ Make two copies of photocopiable page 189. Cut around the shapes and use them for games such as 'Snap' and 'Pairs'.

■ Show the children photocopiable page 190. Can they find the five differences in the second picture on the page?

■ Ask the children to help the taxi find the right route home to its garage on photocopiable page 191. They can either trace the route with a finger or draw a line with a pencil. Encourage them to move their eyes from left to right as they complete the activity.

THINKING

■ Tell the children to imagine they have a big heavy **axe** in their hands to cut logs of wood. They should swing the axe from over their shoulder as they cut **six** logs for the fire.

■ Ask the children to imagine they are putting **wax** on the furniture to make it shine – smoothing on the wax with a duster, then polishing the wood to make it shine. Encourage them to try this with an adult at home on real furniture.

■ Collect different sizes of **box**. Make an obstacle course with some boxes to climb over, some boxes to crawl through and some boxes to climb in and out of. Time how long it takes the children to complete the obstacle course. Get someone to shout out the time. Can they get faster and faster?

■ Tell the children to imagine it is a very wet and windy day. They are looking for a **taxi** to take them home. Encourage them to jump up and down, waving their arms to try to get a taxi to stop. They should thank the taxi driver, and sit back on the seat. How do they feel now that they are in the taxi? When they have reached their house, they should pay the driver and go inside.

THINKING AND REASONING SKILLS

■ Show the children the picture on photocopiable page 188 and ask them the following questions:

1. What is in the picture?
2. What do you think will happen next?
3. How do we get wood?
4. Who is going to cut up the wood with the axe?
5. What will he use the wood for?
6. What do we use wood for?
7. What do you know of that is made of wood?
8. What else can we do with wood?
9. Do you know of anyone who has a wood-burning fire or cooker?
10. Does wood float or sink?

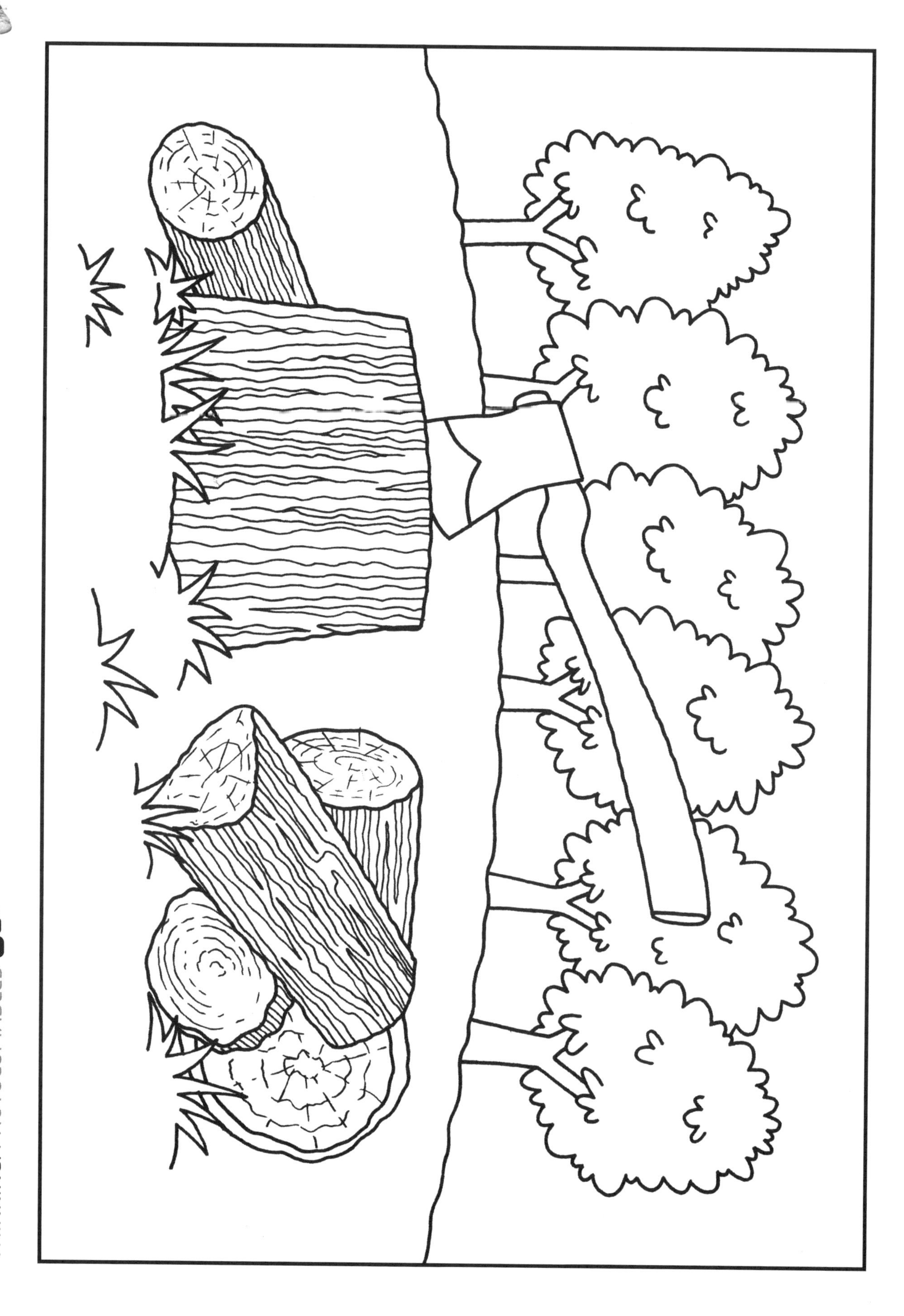

Words containing *x*

Can you guess the words that contain the ***x*** sound?

Answers: box, fox, axe, six, taxi, exit

Spot the difference

Can you find five things that are different in the second picture?

Help the taxi

Help the taxi to get to the garage through the streets.

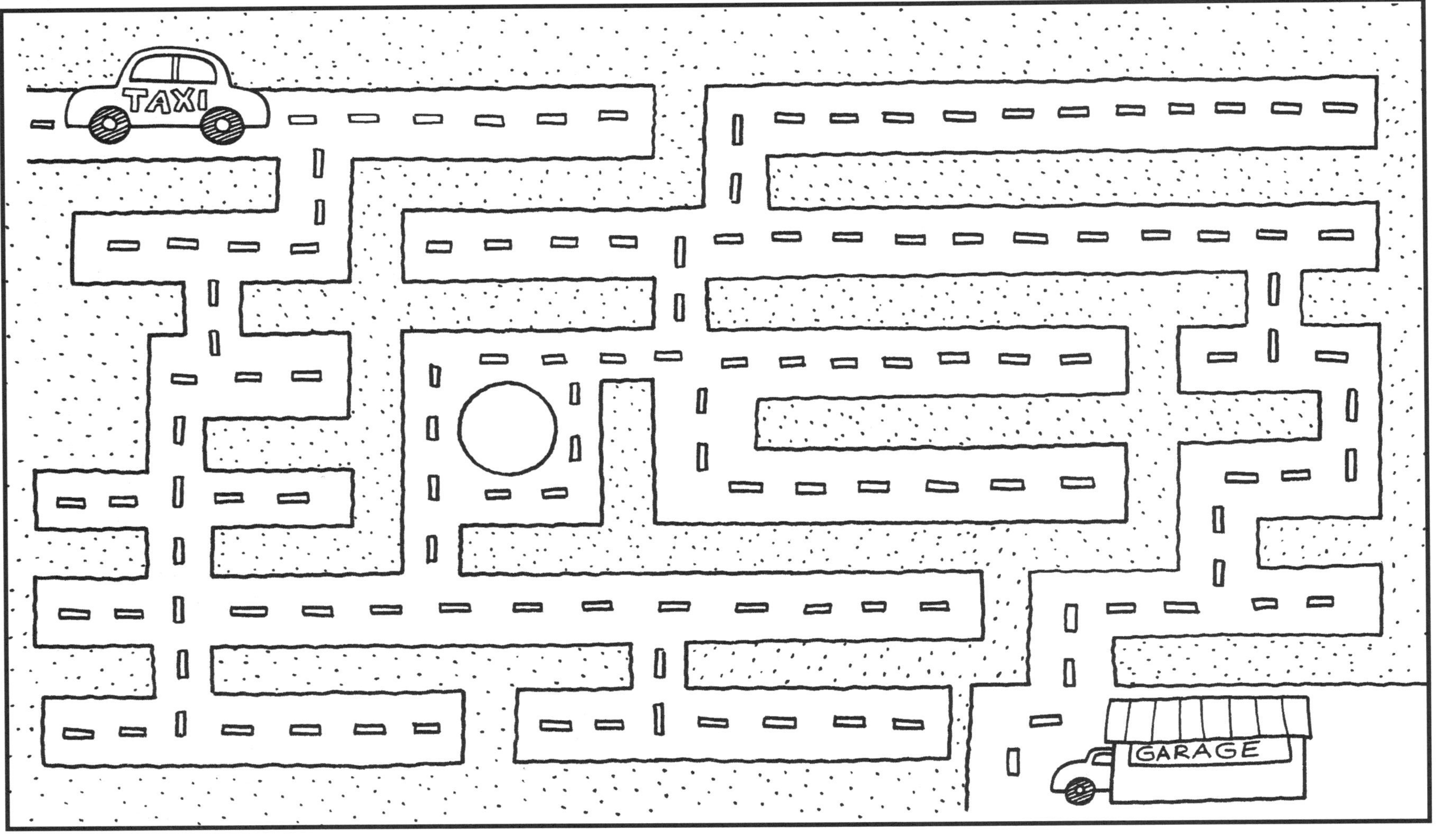

THE y SOUND
(y as in yacht)

PRONUNCIATION GUIDE
To make the **y** sound, open your mouth a little, with the tongue near the top of the mouth. As you make the sound, your tongue touches the sides of your teeth.

LISTENING

WHAT'S ON THE CD
- The rhymes and games for the y sound include:
  - Yankee Doodle Dandy
  - Listening game

RHYMES AND SONGS
- Share rhymes and songs containing the **y** sound.

The Grand Old Duke of York

Oh, the grand old Duke of York,
He had ten thousand men.
He marched them up to the top of the hill,
And he marched them down again.
And when they were up, they were up,
And when they were down, they were down.
And when they were only halfway up,
They were neither up nor down.

Other verses:
They beat their drums to the top of the hill...

They played their pipes to the top of the hill...

They banged their guns to the top of the hill...

I Will Give You a Paper of Pins

I will give you a paper of pins
And that is the way that love begins.
If you will marry, marry, marry, marry,
If you will marry me.

I don't want a paper of pins.
If that is the way love begins.
And I won't marry, marry , marry, marry,
And I won't marry you.

I will give you a dress of red
Stitched all around with golden thread,
If you will marry, marry, marry, marry,
If you will marry me.

I won't accept your dress of red
Stitched all around with golden thread,
And I won't marry, marry , marry, marry,
And I won't marry you.

I've Got One Head

I've got one head,
One nose, too,
One mouth, one chin,
So have you.

I've got two eyes,
Two ears too,
Two arms, two legs,
And so have you.

I've got two hands,
Two thumbs too,
Four fingers on each hand,
And so have you.

If You Should Meet a Crocodile

If you should meet a crocodile,
Don't take a stick and poke him.
Ignore the welcome of his smile,
Be careful not to stroke him.
For as he sleeps upon the Nile,
He thinner gets and thinner.
But whene'r you see a crocodile ,
He's ready for his dinner.

Yankee Doodle Dandy

Yankee Doodle came to London,
Riding on a pony.
He stuck a feather in his cap,
And called it macaroni.

Yankee Doodle keep it up,
Yankee Doodle dandy,
Mind the music and the steps,
And with the girls be handy.

First he bought a porridge pot,
And then he bought a ladle,
And then he trotted home again,
As fast as he was able.

Yankee Doodle keep it up,
Yankee Doodle dandy,
Mind the music and the steps,
And with the girls be handy.

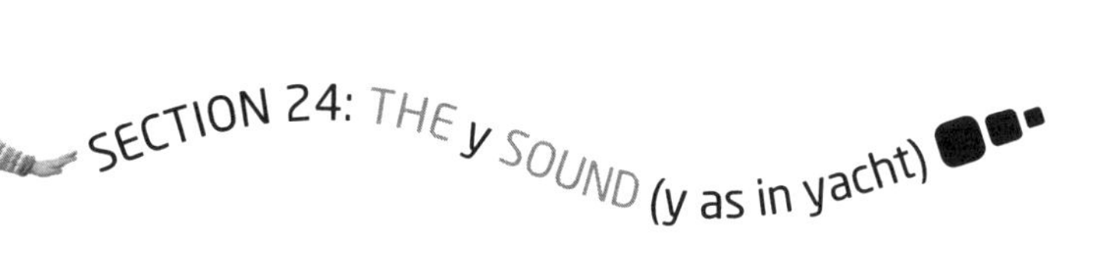

SECTION 24: THE y SOUND (y as in yacht)

ACTIVITIES

Listen to the CD and ask the children if they can guess the missing words in the sentences. The sentences and answers are below.

- The colour of a sunflower is... (**yellow**)
- When I am sleepy, I open my mouth wide and... (**yawn**)
- My grandma is very old but I am very... (**young**)
- My grandpa likes to sail his... (**yacht**)

■ Play an action game: an adult whispers an action to the child, remembering to emphasise the **y** sound. The child then has to act it out. Other children then try to guess the action. This is difficult, so give help and clues, so that the child is successful. For example, actions could include:

- **Yell** out loud.
- **Yawn**.
- Play with a **yo-yo**.
- Sail a **yacht**.
- Be a big scary **yeti**.
- Eat something **yummy**.

■ Look for story books which begin with the **y** sound and read them aloud to your class. For example:

The Youngest Fairy Godmother Ever by Stephen Krensky (Aladdin Paperbacks)
Behind You! by David Pelham (Jonathan Cape Children's Books)
Yummy Yucky by Leslie Patricelli (Walker Books Ltd)
Yes by Jez Alborough (Walker Books Ltd)
You and Me, Little Bear by Martin Waddell and Barbara Firth (Walker Books Ltd)
You Can Do It, Sam by Amy Hest and Anita Jeram (Walker Books Ltd)
You're All My Favourites by Sam McBratney and Anita Jeram (Walker Books Ltd)

■ Look for non-fiction books in the library. You can find books about yaks, yo-yos, yew trees, yachts.
■ Find children's names beginning with the **y** sound, such as Yosef, Yoel, Yannis, Yehudi, Yorick, Yasmin, Yona, Yan, Yanka.
■ Help the children to learn how to use a **yo-yo**.
■ Make a collection of **yellow** toys. Encourage the children to look for yellow objects in picture books.

■ Ask the children if they have tried different flavours of **yoghurt**. Have they have tried different types of yoghurt? (For example, drinking, plain, fruit flavours, fromage frais, Greek.)
■ Break an egg into a container. Look at the white part and the **yellow yolk**. Boil an egg for three minutes, and let the children dip thin strips of toast into the yolk to taste it. (Ensure you are aware of any food allergies or dietary requirements before commencing this activity.)
■ Use **yeast** to make bread. Ask the children if they know what yeast does. Put some yeast into a bowl of warm water (not hot water, which will kill the yeast) and watch what happens. Again, make sure you are aware of any food allergies or dietary requirements beforehand.

EVALUATION

■ These questions are intended to assess the children's ability to hear the **y** sound. Ask them to rub the outside part of their ears before they start to listen.
■ Read the following questions to the children:

1. What sound is at the beginning of these words? yacht, yoghurt, yo-yo, yolk, yellow, yak, you, yawn, yes, year
2. In these groups of three words, which word begins with the **y** sound?
   a) yacht, tent, snore
   b) ant, fig, yawn
   c) child, yo-yo, play
   d) year, jack, house
   e) walk, van, yellow
   f) yes, friend, game
3. Clap when you hear a word with the **y** sound at the beginning:

yacht, yoghurt, sand, yo-yo, tent, yoke, yellow , yak

EXTENSION ACTIVITY

■ As a further challenge for children you can try 'Robot talk'. A list of suggested words is given below.

■ The adult says the word such as 'yes' and then says it in 'Robot talk' /y/e/s/, sounding out the individual sounds. Then repeat this.

■ The child then says the word, for example 'yes'. It may take a few tries to perfect the word.

■ The adult then says the sounds and claps each one, for example /y/e/s/. Then the child joins in.

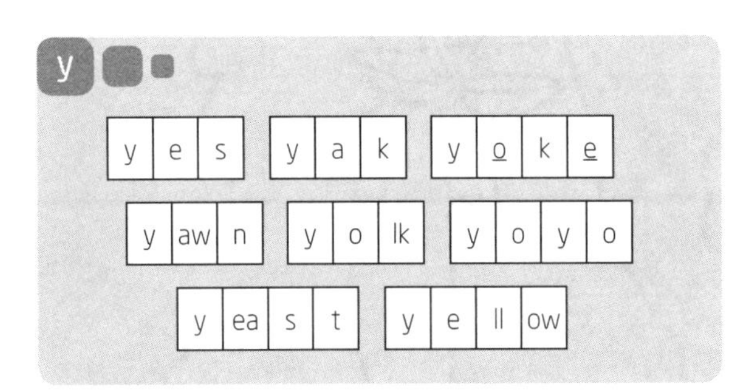

SEEING

■ Show the children photocopiable page 197 and ask them if they can identify the objects beginning with the **y** sound.

■ Make two copies of photocopiable page 197. Cut around the shapes and use them for games such as 'Snap' and 'Pairs'.

■ Ask the children to find the five differences in the second picture on photocopiable page 198.

■ Hand out copies of photocopiable page 199. Ask the children to circle or colour in all the objects that begin with the **y** sound.

THINKING

■ Ask the children to jump up and down like a **yo-yo**, doing big jumps and little jumps.

■ Tell the children they are waking up. They should give a big **yawn** and stretch their whole body, as tall as they can. Then curl up as small as possible and go to sleep. Wake up, yawning and stretching again.

■ Encourage the children to pretend that they have a **yo-yo** in each hand. Make one arm go up and down with the yo-yo. Now make the other hand go up and down. Can they do both hands together?

■ Invite the children to imagine that they are sailing on a **yacht** out on the ocean, bobbing up and down over the big waves. While they are visualising the scene, play some suitable music (for example, 'Fingal's Cave' from the *Hebrides Overture* by Mendelssohn).

■ Ask the children to imagine they are a daffodil bulb under the earth. It is springtime; the sun comes out, and they grow up from the ground to be a **yellow** flower. The wind is blowing, and their head is bobbing in the breeze. As a follow-up, plant daffodil bulbs and watch them grow.

THINKING AND REASONING SKILLS

■ Show the children the picture on photocopiable page 196 and ask them the following questions:

1. What type of boat is in the picture?
2. What is the weather like?
3. What will happen if the yacht begins to sink?
4. What do you call a ship that sinks or runs aground?
5. Is there somebody on the yacht?
6. What will they do if the yacht starts sinking?
7. Do they have a rubber dinghy and lifejackets?
8. Will they swim to safety?
9. Do you know what an island is?
10. What are the trees called?
11. Have you seen these trees where you live?
12. Is the place in the picture hot or cold? How do you know?
13. Can you swim?
14. Do you use armbands or a ring to help you?
15. Can you use them without air in them?
16. Would they help you to float?
17. What three things would you take with you if you were shipwrecked on an island?
18. Who would you want to be with you?
19. How would you feel when you are rescued?

Words beginning with *y*

Can you guess the word beginning with ***y***?

Answers: yacht, yoghurt, yo-yo, yolk, yellow, yawn

Spot the difference

Can you find five things that are different in the second picture?

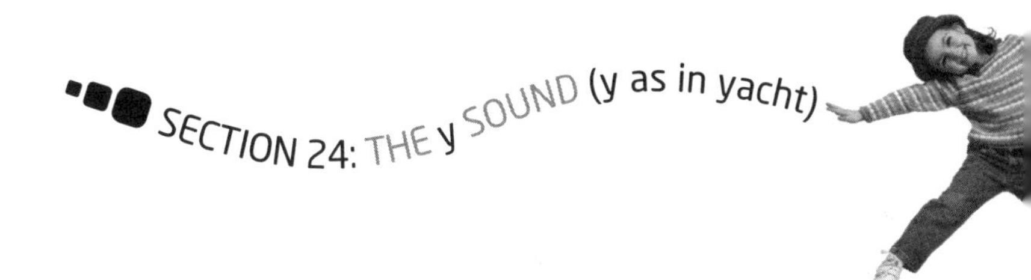

Find the *y*

Circle or colour the things that begin with ***y***.

THE z SOUND

(z as in zebra)

PRONUNCIATION GUIDE

To make the **z** sound, put the tongue at the top of the mouth, behind the teeth. Open the mouth a little, and make the sound at the back of your mouth. Blow out the air.

LISTENING

WHAT'S ON THE CD

- The rhymes and games for the z sound include:
  - Fuzzy Wuzzy Was a Bear
  - Listening game

RHYMES AND SONGS

- Share rhymes and songs containing the **z** sound.

If You Ever, Ever, Ever Meet a Grizzly Bear

If you ever, ever, ever meet a grizzly bear,
You must never, never, never ask him where
He is going,
Or what he is doing;
For if you ever, ever dare
To stop a grizzly bear,
You will never meet another grizzly bear.

We're Going to the Zoo to See a Kangaroo

We're going to the zoo to see a kangaroo,
We're going to the zoo to see a kangaroo, and a lion too,
We're going to the zoo.
The monkeys sing and climb,
They know it's feeding time,
The polar bears and seals,
Enjoy their fishy meals.
We're going to the zoo to see a kangaroo,
We're going to the zoo to see a kangaroo, and a lion too,
We're going to the zoo.

Zany, Zany Addlepate

Zany, Zany Addlepate
Go to bed early,
Get up late,
Zany, Zany Addlepate.

Zum, Gali Gali Gali

Zum gali gali gali, Zum gali gali.
Zum gali gali gali. Zum gali gali.
The pioneer lives for his work,
The work exists for the pioneer.

Zum gali gali gali, Zum gali gali.
Zum gali gali gali. Zum gali gali.
Peace for all nations,
All nations for Peace.

Z is for Zebra

Z is for Zebra,
It's black, striped with white.
Or else white with black stripes,
I'm not sure which is right.

Fuzzy Wuzzy Was a Bear

Fuzzy Wuzzy was a bear,
Fuzzy Wuzzy had no hair,
Fuzzy Wuzzy didn't care.
Fuzzy Wuzzy wasn't fuzzy, was he?

Sneezing

Sneeze on a Monday, sneeze for danger;
Sneeze on a Tuesday, meet a stranger;
Sneeze on a Wednesday, get a letter;
Sneeze on a Thursday, something better;
Sneeze on a Friday, sneeze for sorrow;
Sneeze on Saturday, see your sweetheart
tomorrow.

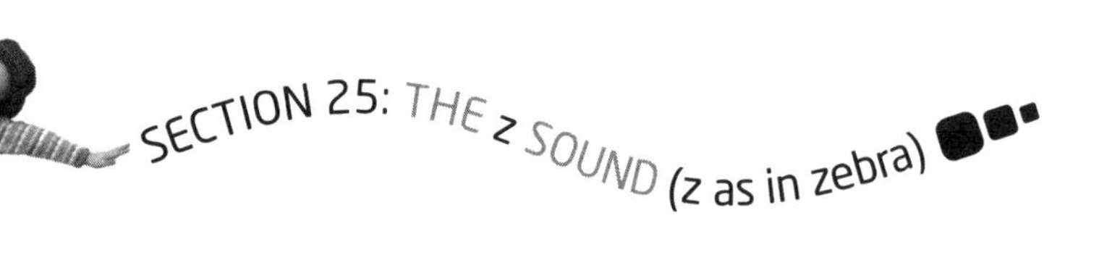

SECTION 25: THE z SOUND (z as in zebra)

ACTIVITIES

Listen to the CD and ask the children if they can guess the missing words in the sentences. The sentences and answers are below.
- What am I? I have four legs, I look like a horse but I have black and white stripes. (**zebra**)
- My anorak closes up with a... (**zip**)

- Play an action game: an adult whispers an action to the child, remembering to emphasise the **z** sound. The child then has to act it out. Other children then try to guess the action. This is difficult, so give help and clues, so that the child is successful. For example, actions could include:
  - Pull up a **zip** in your jacket.
  - Pull up a **zip** in your boots.
  - **Buzz** around like a bee.
  - Draw **zigzag** lines with your hand.
- Look for story books which begin with the **z** sound and read them aloud to your class. For example:

Zug the Bug by Colin Hawkins and Jacqui Hawkins (Pat and Pals Ltd)
Zaza's Baby Brother by Lucy Cousins (Walker Childrens Paperbacks)
Zed's Bread by Mick Manning and Brita Granstrom (Walker Books Ltd)
The Wonderful Wizard of Oz by L Frank Baum (Penguin)
Dear Zoo by Rod Hunt (Campbell Books)

- Look for non-fiction books in the library. You can find books about zoo animals (including zebras) and road safety (zebra crossings)
- Find children's names beginning with the **z** sound, such as Zebedee, Zak, Zachariah, Zamir, Zoltan, Zareb, Zoe, Zara, Zafirah, Zita, Zohar.
- Collect things which have a **zip**. Encourage the children to practise closing a zip on a jacket.
- Help the children fold a narrow sheet of paper (about 10cm wide) in a **zigzag** pattern (a concertina shape, by folding one way, then the other). Help the children cut or tear little pieces from the long side of the folded edges. Unfold the paper, to see their design.
- Encourage the children to play with a toy **zoo** or make a zoo for plastic zoo animals. You may be able to borrow one from your local toy library.

EVALUATION

- These questions are intended to assess the children's ability to hear the **z** sound. Ask them to rub the outside part of their ears before they start to listen.
- Read the following questions to the children:
  1. What sound is at the beginning of these words?
     zebra, zip, zoo, zigzag, zoom
  2. In these groups of three words, which word begins with the **z** sound?
     a) zebra, hiss, sack
     b) car, drive, zoom
     c) zoo, band, elephant
     d) sun, zebra, hand
     e) wish, fairy, zip
     f) ship, sand, zigzag
  3. Clap when you hear a word with the **z** sound at the beginning:
     zebra, sand, zip, zoo, room, zigzag, tooth, zoom

EXTENSION ACTIVITY

- As a further challenge for children you can try 'Robot talk'. A list of suggested words is given below.
  - The adult says the word such as 'zip' and then says it in 'Robot talk' /z/i/p/, sounding out the individual sounds. Then repeat this.
  - The child then says the word, for example 'zip'. It may take a few tries to perfect the word.

■ The adult then says the sounds and claps each one, for example /z/i/p/. Then the child joins in.

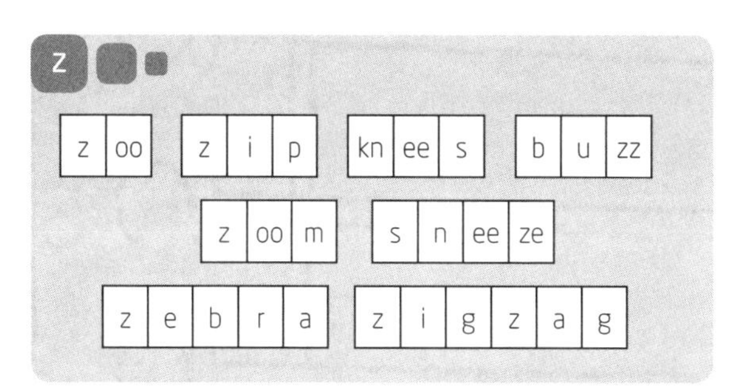

SEEING

■ Show the children photocopiable page 205 and ask them if they can identify the objects containing the **z** sound.
■ Make two copies of photocopiable page 205. Cut around the shapes and use them for games such as 'Snap' and 'Pairs'.
■ Show the children photocopiable page 206. Ask them to point to the zebras in the array of objects on the page.
■ Hand out copies of photocopiable page 207. Ask the children to join the dots to make the shape of a zebra.

THINKING

■ Draw **zigzag** lines on the ground with chalk. Ask the children to walk along the lines, without falling off.
■ Invite the children to make a large **zigzag** pattern in the air with their arm. Start as high as they can. Use one arm, and then the other arm. Try both arms together.
■ Listen to the music of **Zorba's** dance (you can find this in compilations of Greek music). Encourage the children to dance to the music, getting faster and faster.
■ Tell the children to imagine they are going on a visit to the **zoo**. Which favourite animal will they go to see? Ask: *Could you play with your animal or is it dangerous? What will you feed to your animal? How do zoos keep people safe from the dangerous animals?* If any of the children have been to a zoo or safari park, invite them to tell the other children about it.
■ Encourage the children to imagine they are driving a fast car down a hill with **zigzag** streets, steering the car around the zigzags. If possible, show them a picture of Lombard Street in San Francisco which has zigzags.

THINKING AND REASONING SKILLS

Show the children the picture on photocopiable page 204 and ask them the following questions:

1. What animal is in the picture?
2. Can he escape?
3. Why not?
4. Who feeds the zebra?
5. What does a zebra eat?
6. Do you think that animals should be kept in a zoo?
7. Where should they live?
8. Would you like to be in a cage, with people looking in at you? Why/why not?
9. If you were an animal, what animal would you like to be? Where would you live? What would you eat? Act at being your animal, making the animal's noise. Can the other children guess what animal you are?

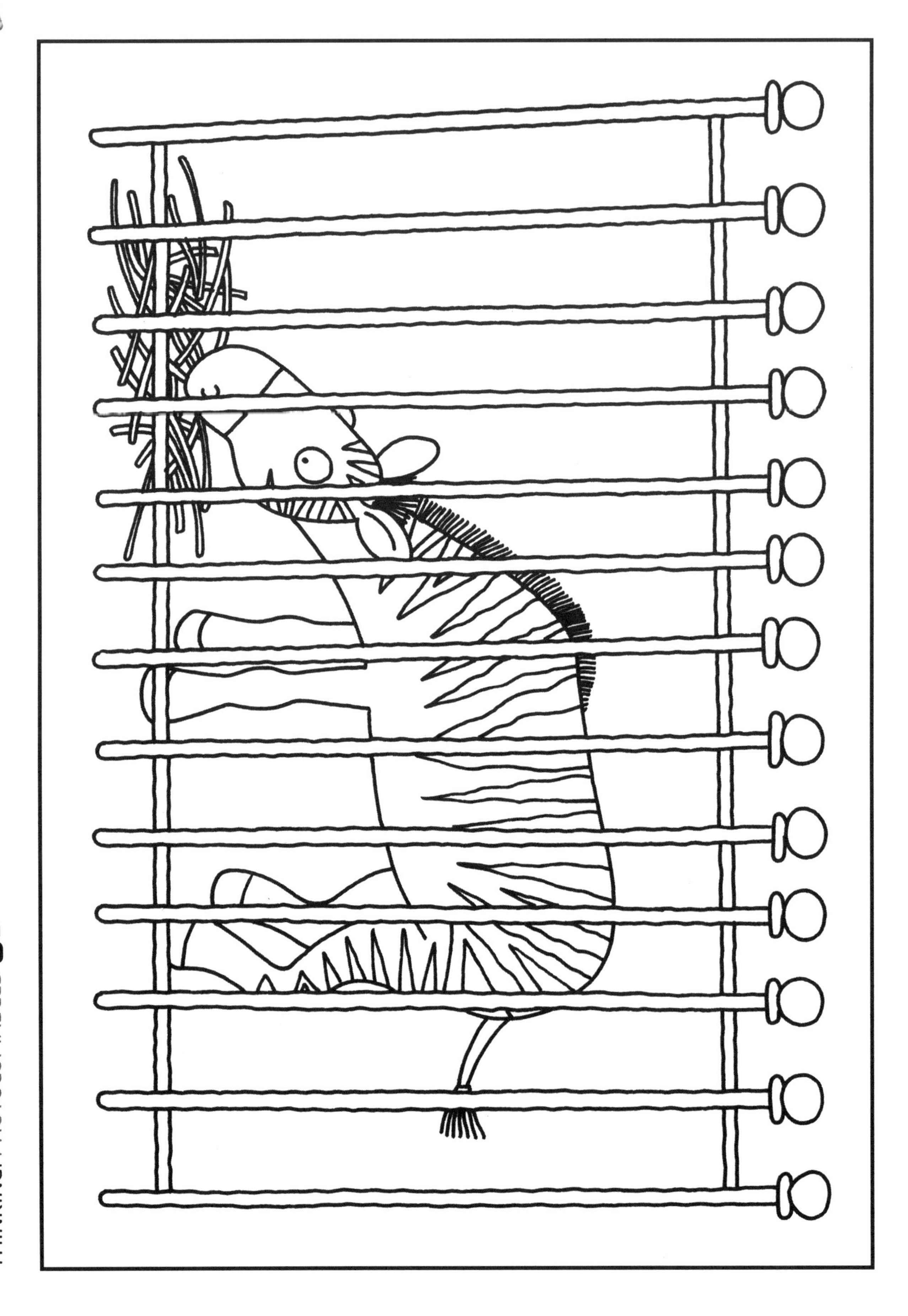

Words containing the *z* sound

Can you say the words that contain the **z** sound?

Answers: zebra, zip, zigzag lines, zebra crossing, grizzly bear, sneeze, knees, fizzy drink

Find the zebras

Can you point to the zebras?

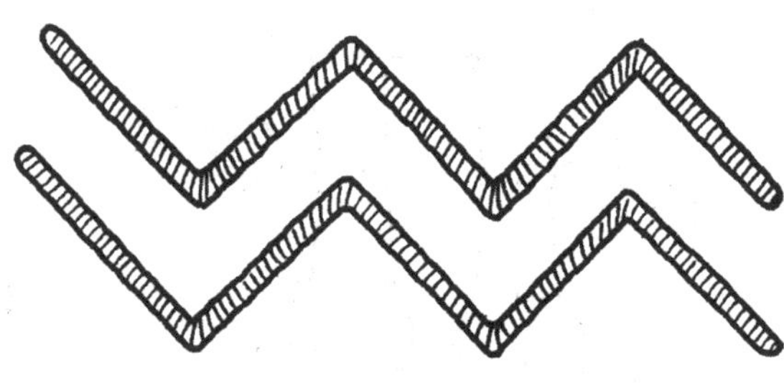

Dot-to-dot zebra

Join up the dots to make the shape of a zebra.
Have you ever seen a zebra in a zoo or a safari park?